The Pocket Guide to the
Coastal Birds

of Britain
and
Europe

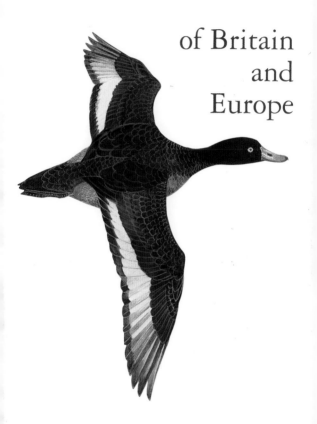

Peter Hayman & Rob Hume

MITCHELL BEAZLEY

The Pocket Guide to the Coastal Birds of Britain and Europe
by Peter Hayman and Rob Hume
First published in Great Britain in 2005 by Mitchell Beazley, an
imprint of Octopus Publishing Group Ltd, 2–4 Heron Quays,
London E14 4JP

ISBN 1 84533 073 0
A CIP record for this book is available from the British Library.
Set in Garamond and Gill Sans
Colour reproduction by Alliance Graphics, London
Printed and bound in china by Toppan Printing Company Limited

Commissioning Editor: Vivien Antwi | Executive Art Editor: Yasia Williams
Managing Editor: Juanne Branquinho | Editor: John Woodward
Design: Kenny Grant | Production: Gary Hayes

Bird size key

145–160cm 57–63in

Each bird's length, laid flat, from bill to tail tip
is given in centimetres and inches. As a visual
guide, a silhouette shows the relative size for
each in comparison with a town pigeon
(31–35cm/12–14in). For smaller birds (59cm/
23in and under), the scale is double that used for
larger birds (60cm/23.5in and over).

Habitat key

Symbols show the main habitats in which each bird can be found:
these are shorthand guides, not an exhaustive list.

OPEN SEA/OFFSHORE		MUDFLATS, CREEKS	
INSHORE/SHELTERED BAYS		ESTUARY/SALTMARSH	
CLIFFS, ROCKS, ISLANDS		COASTAL LAGOONS, MARSH	
SHINGLE/STONY BEACHES		GRASSLAND/WASTE	
SANDY BEACH/DUNES		COASTAL URBAN AREAS	

Contents

Introduction
Rob Hume

Birdwatching at the coast is always something to take advantage of, whenever the oportunity arises. Living at the coast is a great bonus for people interested in birds; those of us who live far inland will try to get to the sea as often as possible, as most people do.

Water always adds another dimension to any habitat and brings in a greater number and variety of birds. On the sea coast, numbers can be tremendous: some large estuaries have tens of thousands of wading birds and wildfowl in autumn, winter, and spring, while some sea cliffs are home to tens of thousands of breeding seabirds.

Many wading birds, ducks, and geese fly north in summer to take advantage of the short but rich breeding season in the Arctic. They must return south early in the autumn to find a safe, more temperate refuge for the rest of the year. The coasts of Europe are especially good for such birds, which come to spend the winter from almost all over the Northern Hemisphere.

This book includes other birds that, while not specific to the coast, are characteristic of many days out near the sea: some breed on coastal pools, grasslands or cliffs, while others are seen on coasts while on migration in spring and autumn.

The book is based around magnificent paintings by Peter Hayman. They are the result of years of study in the field and in museums, where he has spent many hours drawing and measuring skins and specimens kept in spirit. They are among the most accurate, as well as most beautiful, ever produced.

Rob Hume

TURNSTONE

The parts of a coastal bird
Helping to understand the descriptions

This book is non-technical, but a few specialist terms are used to describe the patterns on birds. These patterns are created by different coloured feathers, feather edges and feather tips, on the various "feather tracts" that cover the bird's body. Some are obvious, such as "chin" and "throat"; others, such as "tertials", are specific to birds. These terms are few, easily learned, and invaluable for describing patterns with precision. The diagrams below highlight some of the more useful ones, although not all birds have all of the features that have been marked: many are much plainer than this.

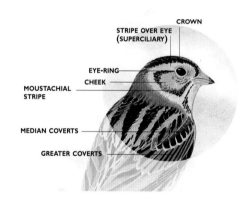

CROWN
STRIPE OVER EYE (SUPERCILIARY)
EYE-RING
CHEEK
MOUSTACHIAL STRIPE
MEDIAN COVERTS
GREATER COVERTS

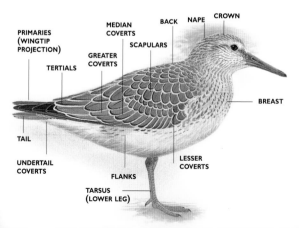

PRIMARIES (WINGTIP PROJECTION)
TERTIALS
MEDIAN COVERTS
GREATER COVERTS
SCAPULARS
BACK
NAPE
CROWN
BREAST
TAIL
UNDERTAIL COVERTS
FLANKS
TARSUS (LOWER LEG)
LESSER COVERTS

What is a coastal bird?
The birds in this book

There are three basic categories of "coastal bird" in this book. Some breed on the coast; others spend the winter there; others appear on habitats that are often found by the coast, such as heaths, rough grassland, and cliffs. Many are migrants in spring and autumn, but so many species can be found on coastlines at some time or another that we have been unable to be exhaustive in our selection.

▲ **Snow bunting**
Breeds on cliffs and tundra, but spends the winter on low-lying coasts

BIRDS OF THE OPEN SEA AND OCEAN

The true coastal birds with which we are concerned include those that are popularly grouped as "seabirds". They live much of their lives at sea, often far from the sight of land, but have to come to land to breed.

They include rare petrels that nest on remote islands, the fulmar that feeds around trawlers but nests on cliff ledges, shearwaters that come to land only at night to avoid predators, and the puffins, razorbills, and guillemots that breed on cliffs but spend most of their lives far offshore.

Terns breed in Europe but migrate south to Africa in the winter. The Arctic tern flies even farther, to feed near the edge of the Antarctic pack-ice. The gulls include several species that nest on the coast, but which may spend the winter around rubbish tips, feeding on fields, or scavenging for food along the beaches of seaside resorts. The skuas are scarce, exciting birds, often stealing food from other birds at sea; they are all migrants to Europe in summer.

DUCKS, GEESE AND SWANS

The wildfowl are birds of water and waterside habitats. Some in this book are true seabirds, such as the scoters and long-tailed duck, while others, such as brent geese, breed far to the north or east and spend the non-breeding season on the coasts of Europe. Some species, such as mallards and Canada geese, are more common around freshwater inland, but are often seen on coastal pools or marshes.

The divers and grebes, and the coot, are not wildfowl, being unrelated to ducks, but they swim on the sea and occur in many coastal areas.

WADERS AND HERONS

The waders include the plovers and sandpipers, the latter an especially varied group including very small and quite large birds. Plovers have short, thick bills with which they pick food from the surface of mud, sand, or soil. Other waders have longer bills of varying shapes for probing into softer mud and sand, or feeding in shallow water. Many of these waders are among the great travellers of the bird world, simply stopping off in Europe as they migrate between their summer ranges in the Arctic and their winter homes in Africa.

◄ **Herring gull**
The common "seagull" of most seaside towns

Herons and egrets are all water birds, not all specifically coastal, but as likely to be seen in coastal marshes and lagoons, or on sheltered estuary creeks, as anywhere else. The greater flamingo breeds in spectacular colonies, mostly on islands in large, shallow, coastal lagoons, but it can be seen in saline lakes along many southern coasts.

LARKS, PIPITS, FINCHES, AND BUNTINGS

The coast is rich in seeds, insects, and other tiny invertebrates, all of which can be exploited by small birds including the shore lark, twite, and snow bunting, which are coastal birds outside the breeding season.

◄ **Curlew**
A large wader, which breeds on moors and hills inland, but comes down to the coast at other times; it can be seen on muddy shores almost all year round

How to identify a coastal bird
Getting to grips with the birds

Some coastal birds are large and easy to identify, given anything like a reasonably good view. The gannet, puffin, and Canada goose, for example, give few problems. Others, such as the swans, can readily be narrowed down to two or three choices.

There are others that are colourful or striking, and seem easy to identify, but which can be more difficult than expected in the context of a day out on the coast. Many coastal habitats are wide open and extensive: the marshes and estuaries of Europe can be wild, remote, dramatic places with fast-rising tides and ever-changing weather and light. Birds in such places are apt to be difficult. A huge area of mud at low tide, gleaming silver under a bright sky, can be covered with dots of various sizes: wading birds, of several species, but which ones? Against the light their colours are hard to see; in such open places they are hard to approach and quick to fly away. Birdwatching in such habitats can be challenging, but given a determination to succeed it can be very rewarding.

HIGH-TIDE GATHERINGS

There are ways to improve your chances of seeing birds closely and well enough to identify them. Estuaries, for example, have regular high-tide roosts at which all the birds gather to rest and wait until the tide recedes, when they can once again disperse over the beach to feed. These roosts may be on the shore or on nearby fields or pools. If you get to know these places, and use your fieldcraft to get close without disturbing the birds, you will see them in ideal conditions. There are bird reserves on many European coasts that offer such experiences.

Coastal pools and marshes, also often nature reserves, are excellent places for all kinds of birds, from waders to ducks, geese, and birds of prey. You can usually see them closer here than out on the open shore, greatly improving your chances of telling them all apart.

◀ **Green sandpiper**
Waders show distinctive patterns in flight, such as this dark-winged bird with a bold white rump – but good views are essential

SEABIRD COLONIES AND SEAWATCHING

A good way to see birds close-up is to visit a colony of breeding seabirds on a cliff between March and early August, where there may be kittiwakes, fulmars, herring gulls, guillemots, and others in abundance. Most birds are surprisingly approachable in such circumstances.

▲ **Common gulls**
Adult, immature, and seasonal plumages offer a range of colours and patterns for just one species; it takes time to sort these out

Colonies on flatter, lower shores, such as those of terns on sand and shingle, are not easy to see. The birds are far too easily disturbed, unless the colonies are on nature reserves provided with hides. It is better to watch birds such as terns – as well as gulls, skuas, and passing shearwaters and gannets – from a headland, especially in spring and autumn. This is a popular pastime, called "seawatching", but it requires great patience, a good telescope, and probably the ability to watch day after day at most places until conditions are just right to bring many birds close to the shore: perhaps an autumn gale might do the trick. Seawatching is not easy because the birds are passing by on migration, or at least on their way to or from a colony, and are unlikely to return; there is just one chance to identify them. Despite this, seawatching can be exciting and rewarding.

▼ **Scaup**
Typically a sea-duck of inshore waters, but often found on pools by the coast or inland, where it may be confused with the commoner tufted duck

The coastal habitats
Where to find coastal birds

DISTRIBUTION
Coastal birds breed in areas marked RED; they spend the winter, or are seen on migration, in areas marked BLUE; they can be seen all year in areas marked PURPLE. Some breed in the north in late May, June, and July; they may be seen in "winter" areas from late July to almost the end of May.

We have indicated the habitats used by each species with symbols.

OPEN SEA/OFFSHORE
The Atlantic, North Sea, and Mediterranean, far from the shore.

INSHORE/SHELTERED BAYS
The sea visible from the shore, especially from headlands near which some seabirds can be seen moving to feeding areas, or on migration.

CLIFFS, ROCKS, ISLANDS
Many seabirds breed on sheer cliffs above the edge of the sea; others on offshore rocks and islands.

SHINGLE/STONY BEACHES
Difficult habitats with little food, exploited by few coastal birds.

SANDY BEACH/DUNES
Open sandy bays – the beaches we like for holidays – are not usually productive, but some birds feed or rest there if undisturbed. Dune systems are richer and attract many small birds on migration.

MUDFLATS, CREEKS
Open mudflats, covered by the tide twice every day, are richer than the best farmland, with vast numbers of tiny snails, worms, and other invertebrates. These are feeding grounds for tens of thousands of wildfowl and wading birds.

Bar-tailed godwits ▼
Wading birds of muddy beaches

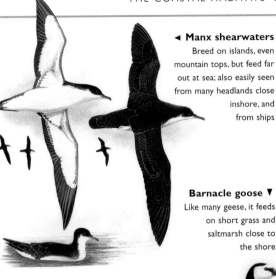

◄ Manx shearwaters
Breed on islands, even mountain tops, but feed far out at sea; also easily seen from many headlands close inshore, and from ships

Barnacle goose ▼
Like many geese, it feeds on short grass and saltmarsh close to the shore

☒ ESTUARY/SALTMARSH

Rivers meet the sea in estuaries, which may open onto mudflats, or have saltmarsh at their edges and dunes, sandbanks, and shingle bars at their mouths.

COASTAL LAGOONS, MARSH

Along many coasts are marshy areas, frequently with reedbeds and shallow pools, where birds feed and nest on shingly islands.

GRASSLAND/WASTE

Many kinds of grassland, from old grazing marsh to improved fields, as well as rough grassland on islands or at the tops of cliffs. Many coasts have "waste" ground around buildings, industrial sites, holiday homes, and so on, as well as golf courses and other open spaces. Many birds exploit these places; not all of them are specific to coasts, but being adjacent to the shore they can be excellent.

COASTAL URBAN AREAS

Towns, harbours, piers, promenades, ferry terminals, industrial sites of all kinds, and even sewage outflows come under this category. A surprising number of species can be encountered in such places.

Mute Swan
Cygnus olor

Flight ▼
Outstretched neck, short tail and legs give unbalanced look; wings make loud throbbing

Juvenile ▼
Grey-brown with whiter wings, becoming patched white with age; grey-and-black bill

Adult ▼
All white; downtilted orange-and-black bill; wings often raised

145–160cm 57–63in

DISTRIBUTION
Widespread breeding bird on lakes, rivers; all year on sheltered coasts, estuaries, marshes, and lagoons

IDENTIFICATION All white except for the black-and-orange bill. Pointed tail and downtilted bill distinguish from other swans. Immatures are browner and blotchier than those of other species. Short, trumpeting snorts and hisses; throbbing wings in flight.

HABITAT Lakes, reservoirs, town ponds and rivers, quiet coasts.

BEHAVIOUR Forms non-breeding flocks on rivers and lakes, but nesting pairs drive others from their territory and can be aggressive towards people who approach too closely. In eastern Europe forms large flocks, and is much wilder, shy, and quick to fly off.

◄ Bill details
Female (top) has smaller black knob than male; immature (bottom) lacks knob until two or three years old

Bewick's Swan
Cygnus columbianus

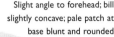

▼ Head and bill details
Slight angle to forehead; bill slightly concave; pale patch at base blunt and rounded

ADULT

JUVENILE

115–130cm 45–51 in

DISTRIBUTION
Breeds on Arctic tundra; in autumn and winter locally on floods, fields, lakes, reservoirs, and coastal marshes

◄ Adult
All white; holds head neck rather erect with bill horizontal; short, square tail kept low on water

IDENTIFICATION A beautiful swan, using loud, bubbling, bugling, and honking calls freely, in contrast with the mute swan. Not always easy to tell from whooper swan unless its smaller size can be judged, but has a less wedge-shaped head and less yellow on the bill, in a rounder, less triangular shape.

HABITAT Marshes, floods, farmland.

BEHAVIOUR Bewick's and whooper swans are more agile on the ground than mute swan, and often occur far from open water, behaving more like geese. Social, rather noisy, and demonstrative birds that feed readily on open, dry ground.

▼ Juvenile and adult
Juvenile dull greyish, becomes whiter by end of winter; adult all white

Whooper Swan
Cygnus cygnus

Adult ▶
All white except for short black legs, black-and-yellow bill. Tail short and square. Whooper (left) bigger than Bewick's (right)

Flight ▲
Lacks throbbing sound in flight

◀ Bill details
Whooper (left) has longer, more triangular yellow patch than Bewick's (right and bottom) on flatter bill

145–160cm 57–63in

DISTRIBUTION
Local breeder on northern lakes; in autumn and winter locally on fields, floods, lakes, coastal marshes

IDENTIFICATION   Whooper swan is a bigger bird than Bewick's, with a longer, flatter head and bill, and louder, more trumpeting calls. It has a shorter, squarer tail and holds its head and bill more horizontally than mute swan.

HABITAT   Whoopers from Iceland move south in winter to Britain and Ireland, where they feed with other swans on fields and shallow floods; others from Scandinavia winter in the Low Countries.

BEHAVIOUR   Whooper swans walk more easily than mutes and take to the air more quickly if disturbed. At some reserves they may be seen closely from hides, but they are shy, wary birds.

▼ Juvenile and adults
Juvenile (left) dull greyish; shape of pale bill patch distinguishes it from similar young Bewick's

Bean Goose
Anser fabalis

Two forms ▼
Tundra race (top) has small bill and short neck; forest race (lower) has big bill and long neck

Adult ▲
Overall dark impression from head to wingtips, paler on chest and belly

Adult ▲
Dark brown, with deep, liver-brown head and neck; sharp pale bars above; pale orange legs

IDENTIFICATION Attractive goose, crisply marked on dark body. Juveniles less neatly marked. Identified in mixed flocks by dark appearance, especially on head and neck, and long-faced look of longer-billed form, which breeds in forest clearings in north Scandinavia. Pattern recalls pink-footed goose, but bill band and legs orange, not pink. Deep calls lack high double notes of pink-footed goose.

HABITAT Prefers arable land and rough grass near the coast.

BEHAVIOUR Generally wild and shy, but may mix with other geese, especially white-fronted.

69–88cm 27–35in

DISTRIBUTION Rare breeder in far north; autumn to spring very local but common in Low Countries on fields, marshes, low-lying areas near coast

Bill details ▼
Forest race has wide orange band on long bill; tundra race (right) has much less orange on squat bill

Tail ▲
Note broad grey band on tail, compared with narrow band on pink-footed goose

Pink-footed Goose
Anser brachyrhynchus

Flight pattern ▶
Forewings bluish-grey, not so pale as greylag, but greyer than those of other geese; typical goose white patch around tail

64–76cm 25–30in

DISTRIBUTION
Breeds on high tundra in Iceland and Svalbard; autumn to spring on fields, grassland, coastal marshes

IDENTIFICATION A medium-large goose, with a round, dark head, short, dark bill, and neatly barred, greyish back. Pink legs not always obvious at long range or in poor light; they may be pale or deep, intense pink. A chorus of calls from a flock contains deep, honking notes interspersed with distinctive, high-pitched *wink-wink* calls.

HABITAT Pink-footed geese have greatly increased in Britain and the Low Countries in recent decades, with better protection of both breeding and wintering areas. In winter they like farmland, usually close to the coast or large reservoirs where they can safely spend the night away

▼ Adult and juvenile
Adult (left) neatly lined on blue-grey back; pink band on short bill; pink legs

JUVENILE

◄ Juvenile
Less neatly barred above and less grey than adult (far left), but still shows distinct round, dark head against pale chest

▼ Tail pattern
Narrow central dark band

from land predators such as foxes. They feed on surplus root crops, sugar beet tops and other arable waste, as well as grass and cereals.

BEHAVIOUR Genuinely wild geese, much more wary than introduced greylag geese and Canada geese, and usually hard to approach. They feed in dense flocks by day, then move to the coast or freshwater refuges in the evening, often flying many miles in long lines, V-shapes, and chevrons, often arriving at their roosts after dark.

At long range ▼
Note rounded shape, short neck, small, dark, round head with small bill; pink legs obvious only at close range

UNDERSIDE

White-fronted Goose
Anser albifrons

64–78cm 25–31in

DISTRIBUTION
Breeds Russia,
Greenland; autumn
to spring on
marshes, grasslands
near coasts, or in
wide river valleys

IDENTIFICATION Less shapely and elegant than bean goose or pink-footed goose, but more contrasty in colour, with white facial blaze and bright leg and bill colours. There are two forms, sometimes treated as two separate species, but they can be hard to tell apart, especially at a distance or in poor light when, like all geese, they can look dark and drab. Colours and patterns are best seen in sunshine, which may pick out the pink bill of the Russian race or the orange bill of the darker Greenland form, which winters mostly in Scotland and Ireland. Both have loud yodelling

GREENLAND RACE

RUSSIAN RACE

Racial variation ▲
Greenland race (top) has
orange bill, darker body;
Russian birds have pink bills;
juvenile (right) lacks white blaze
and black bars on belly

JUVENILE

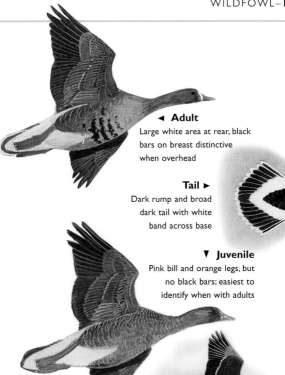

◄ Adult
Large white area at rear, black bars on breast distinctive when overhead

Tail ►
Dark rump and broad dark tail with white band across base

▼ Juvenile
Pink bill and orange legs, but no black bars; easiest to identify when with adults

▲ Upperside
Grey patch on outer wing less extensive than on greylag

calls, without the high *wink-wink* notes of a pink-footed goose, the deep bass tones of a bean goose, or the harder rattle of the greylag.

HABITAT Russian white-fronted geese favour grass fields, where they feed in larger flocks than Greenland breeders, which prefer saltmarshes and wilder, often higher areas.

BEHAVIOUR Most feed on grassy areas and marshland close to water, especially estuaries, to which they fly each evening for a safe night roost. In Britain and Ireland most flocks are now small, but in the Low Countries they can be seen in tens of thousands in favoured places. These huge flocks are quite wary, and quick to move off if disturbed.

Greylag Goose
Anser anser

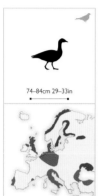

74–84cm 29–33in

Flight ►
Prominent pale grey forewing, above and below, makes large head look rather dark

Adult, all year ▼
Sexes alike; large, pale brown head, greyer body neatly barred above; some have tiny white face patch

DISTRIBUTION
Winter visitors from Iceland to NW Europe, where fewer resident; many introduced into lowland areas

IDENTIFICATION The largest "grey" goose with the heaviest head and bill, less agile than other geese, but still impressive on the wing. Large head and bill distinctive, but bill, leg, and wing colours, and voice, are best clues. Calls are deep and resonant, but more nasal and rattling than musical or honking in quality.

HABITAT Coastal marshes and farmland with grass or cereal crops; also shallow lagoons and gravel pits. Many introduced into farmland areas, often mixing with Canada geese.

BEHAVIOUR Winter visitors from the north are wild and shy, forming large, dramatic flocks, but introduced birds around lakes are often quite tame.

Juvenile ►
Duller bill and legs than adult, and less neatly barred body

◄ Feeding
Feeds in flocks, leaning forward, moving slowly across grass or arable fields

Canada Goose
Branta canadensis

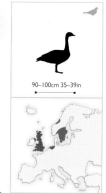

90–100cm 35–39in

Flight ▲
Large, long neck, swan-like shape; big white patch near tail, pale breast, white throat against black head and neck

On ground ▼
Large, barred, brown goose with white undertail and pale breast; black head and neck with broad white chinstrap

DISTRIBUTION
Local, common in UK, near freshwater of all kinds, coastal pools, sometimes marshes

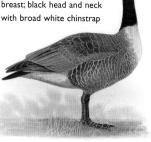

On water ▼
Forward-leaning, head erect, tail up; big white "stern", pale chest

IDENTIFICATION Large, brown-, black-and-white goose with black bill and legs, no bright colour. Bold white throat

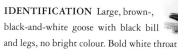

band or chinstrap shows up against black head. Black neck does not extend to breast (unlike barnacle and brent geese). Breast obviously pale buff to white. Loud, honking calls.

HABITAT Originally introduced around ornamental parkland lakes, it has spread to reservoirs, flooded gravel pits, adjacent fields, and floods. Some migrate in autumn to estuaries, coastal marshes.

BEHAVIOUR A social goose, often mixing with introduced greylag geese, but otherwise tending to keep to pure flocks of Canadas. It feeds on grassy areas, but also in shallows, up-ending like swans. Flies in long lines and V-shapes; flocks make noisy chorus.

Barnacle Goose
Branta leucopsis

WHITE-FACED ADULT

BUFF-FACED VARIANT

◀ **Adult**
White face with dark eye patch unique, combined with black breast, white belly, white rear end

58–70cm 23–28in

DISTRIBUTION
Breeds in Arctic; visits small parts of Ireland, N Britain, and Low Countries in winter

IDENTIFICATION A highly social goose, feeding and flying in dense, irregular packs and lines. Beautiful, contrasty plumage; black breast recalls brent goose, but the large white face is unmistakable in a reasonable view. Flocks make a quite unmusical but rhythmic chorus of loud, sharp, barking calls.

HABITAT Coastal fields, marshes, estuaries, lakes near sea. Birds from Greenland winter in western Scotland and Ireland, on islands or near large estuaries. Svalbard breeders go to the Solway Firth. Larger numbers from Siberia go to the Netherlands.

BEHAVIOUR Large flocks, often close to or mixed with pink-footed geese or, especially in the Netherlands, white-fronted geese, feed in wide, open, lowland fields by day or on moonlit evenings. They are shy, wary, and quick to take flight, especially in the shooting season, although they may be more approachable later in the spring. They feed with an easy walk, looking quite long-legged.

◄ Flight pattern
Looks grey, black in front and on lower back, with broad white band above tail; white face usually easy to see

◄ Adult
Neat barring above and gleaming white underside distinctive; juvenile duller, bars less neat

▼ Flight
Barred upperwing looks more uniform lead-grey from a distance, darker towards the leading edge, unlike greylag or pink-footed goose

UNDERSIDE

UPPERSIDE

▲ Feeding action
Typical horizontal, forward-leaning goose shape with head angled down on thick, velvety neck

Relaxed posture ►
More upright body, head withdrawn into shoulders; when alarmed, raises long neck

Brent Goose
Branta bernicla

▼ **Flight impressions**
Long-winged, short-necked, dark with white stern

55–62cm 22–24in

DISTRIBUTION
Breeds in Siberia, spends winter in North Sea area; pale-bellied birds from Greenland winter in Ireland, NE England

IDENTIFICATION Although only mallard-sized, looks bigger, heavier, and broader-winged, partly owing to dark colours. The black of the head and neck, marked by a small splash of white, is more extensive than on barnacle or Canada geese, and the upperside is much darker, scarcely barred except on juveniles. Calls are deep, croaking but attractive *krronk-krronk* notes, often in chorus from a flock.

HABITAT Muddy estuaries are essential, backed by saltmarsh with deep creeks and quiet tidal rivers, pastures, or cereal fields; increasingly tame and more numerous, even on grassy areas by the shore close to towns or marinas.

BEHAVIOUR A duck-like goose, swimming a lot more than most other geese, often up-ending to feed; also feeds in quite dense flocks on farmland. Flies in long lines or irregular groups.

▲ **Immatures**
Juveniles are barred on wings; no neck patch until midwinter or spring

On water ►
Looks squat, high-tailed, short-necked; big, white tail end conspicuous at great distance

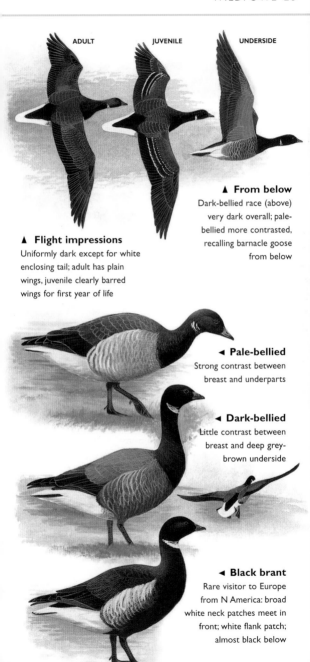

ADULT   **JUVENILE**   **UNDERSIDE**

▲ **From below**
Dark-bellied race (above) very dark overall; pale-bellied more contrasted, recalling barnacle goose from below

▲ **Flight impressions**
Uniformly dark except for white enclosing tail; adult has plain wings, juvenile clearly barred wings for first year of life

◄ **Pale-bellied**
Strong contrast between breast and underparts

◄ **Dark-bellied**
Little contrast between breast and deep grey-brown underside

◄ **Black brant**
Rare visitor to Europe from N America: broad white neck patches meet in front; white flank patch; almost black below

Shelduck
Tadorna tadorna

Distant view ▶
Looks striking white even at very long range: may be missed in gull flock

55–65cm 22–26in

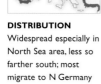

DISTRIBUTION
Widespread especially in North Sea area, less so farther south; most migrate to N Germany in summer, to moult

IDENTIFICATION Adults effectively unmistakable if seen well; even at a great distance their whiteness, upright stance, and goose-like walk (or buoyant, tail-up shape when swimming) are characteristic. Juveniles can be confusing, with dull bills and nondescript plumage; they may be dismissed as hybrid farmyard escapes, but their largely white bodies provide a useful clue. Calls include shrill, squeaky whistling and loud, rhythmic, cackling *ga-ga-ga-ga* in flight.

HABITAT Shelducks have become increasingly familiar inland, especially near flooded gravel pits, but remain mostly coastal birds. They like muddy estuaries and sheltered, sandy bays with large, open flats at low tide. Breeding birds favour dunes and bushy places just inland from the beach, where they nest in the shelter of rabbit burrows, under brambles or other low bushes, or in stacks of straw bales.

BEHAVIOUR Out on the mudflats at low tide, shelducks are typically seen in pairs or small groups, feeding by slowly walking forwards and sweeping their broad, flat bills from side to side through the surface of wet mud. In this way they pick up huge numbers of tiny snails and crustaceans, which are filtered from the mud and water by a fine, mesh-like structure inside the bill. After nesting, most adult shelducks leave their well-grown young in "creches" in the care of a few old birds, and fly to the large, shallow bays off northern Germany where they can moult and replace their feathers in safety. Like most ducks they are unable to fly during this process, and a safe refuge is essential.

ADULT MALE

▲ Adult, all year
Green-black head, black bands flanking back, black on wings, but looks shining white at longer range

Sexes differ ►
Male has black head, brilliant red bill with large red basal knob; female has paler face or cheeks, no knob on bill

ADULT FEMALE

◄ Juvenile
Same size and shape as adult, but dull white and pale brown, with dark cap, white face, white underside, pink legs

Unique pattern ►
Mallard and shoveler have green-black head, but neither is so white on body; shoveler has rufous flanks, not breastband

MALE

FEMALE

JUVENILE

Wigeon
Anas penelope

42–50cm 17–20in

DISTRIBUTION
Breeds very locally in N Britain and N Europe; much more widespread and locally numerous in winter

IDENTIFICATION Medium-large, short-billed, short-legged, colourful duck, often seen in dense flocks. Adult males easy to identify; females or young birds best learned when they accompany them. Male teal has a similar pattern, but looks darker than wigeon, with a more lead-grey, less blue-grey body, darker head, and a yellowish rather than bright white patch in front of the black stern. The wigeon's white forewings are obvious in flight, but young males lack these, even after gaining the adult head and body plumage.

◀ **Juvenile in flight**
Similar to female, but duller hindwing

▼ **Feeding males**
Short, dark legs; yellow forehead often obvious

▼ **Female**
Sharply defined white belly against dark breast and flanks

Summer/autumn male ▶
Like female, but redder; still has white forewing patch

◄ Flight patterns
Female dull with dark hindwing, slightly greyer forewing; male has bold white forewing patches

FEMALE

MALE

▼ Shape
Small, neat head well forward, wings pointed, often held well back; pointed tail

FEMALE FROM BELOW

MALE FROM BELOW

▼ Male
Pale forehead against rich brown head; white band on flank often visible; white near tail

Female ▼
Grey-brown to rufous-brown; neat, round head and small, blue-grey bill; little contrast on rear body and tail

The female can be confusing, but lacks the obvious streaks of a female mallard, gadwall, or shoveler; like a gadwall, it has square white belly patches (female mallard is all-dark beneath) and, like a teal, it has short, dark legs, with none of the bright colour of several other ducks. Females make deep, abrupt growling sounds, while males have loud, clear, rising whistles.

HABITAT Wigeons feed on marshes of all kinds, fresh and salt, and on grassy pastures, lakeside banks, and sometimes mudflats.

BEHAVIOUR A highly social bird, often flying in large flocks over coastal marshes, and feeding in dense packs that seem to carpet the ground with their rich colours.

Gadwall
Anas strepera

▼ Adult male
Grey, with faintly browner head, dark bill; note black around tail and white wing patch

▲ Female
Streaked like mallard, but white belly, white on wing, orange sides to bill

46–56cm 18–22in

DISTRIBUTION
Widespread, but very patchily distributed, mostly rather scarce; in Britain tends to be more common in south and east

IDENTIFICATION Almost mallard-sized, elegant duck with steep forehead and slim bill. Wing pattern is evident in flight, but often hidden at other times, as is female's sharply defined white belly, unlike dark body of female mallard. Males in summer resemble heavily blotched females. Calls include a quiet quack from the female and nasal *ehk ehk* calls from the male.

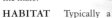

HABITAT Typically a bird of freshwater and coastal marshes, but also saltmarsh creeks and quiet coastal waters.

BEHAVIOUR A social bird where it is common, but often found in ones and twos. It is mostly quiet and unassuming, often keeping close to cover at the water's edge.

▼ Male in flight

Colours of upperwing rarely evident except at close range, but striking white patch on hindwing obvious

▼ Female in flight

White hindwing patch only obvious clue; white belly useful when bird is overhead

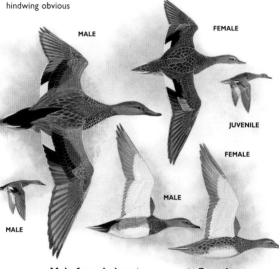

MALE

FEMALE

JUVENILE

FEMALE

MALE

MALE

MALE

Male from below ▲

Neat, compact shape with slim head and bill; bright white underwing striking

▲ Female from below

Less heavy than mallard; white belly recalls wigeon

▼ Male on water

Darker grey than pochard, with grey foreparts, black only at tail end; lead-grey bill distinctive

▼ Female

Dark centre and orange sides to bill useful clues; steep forehead gives different profile from mallard

Teal

Anas crecca

34–38cm 13–15in

DISTRIBUTION
Widespread, but mostly sparsely distributed in summer; more frequent in winter on lakes, marshes

IDENTIFICATION Small, agile, lively duck best identified by size, dark legs and bill, and white line across middle of wing which shows well when it flies. Male also has white stripes along each side of its back; male's head pattern is not easy to see at a distance, when the head and body look dark and uniform. Females are quiet, but males have a bright, ringing *crik-crik* call.

HABITAT All kinds of fresh and brackish water, including coastal marshes and lagoons, and saltmarsh creeks; less often seen on the open sea. Muddy and rushy areas are especially favoured.

BEHAVIOUR A small flock of teals will dash over a marsh and twist and turn like redshanks or golden plovers, looking quick and acrobatic compared with other ducks. They feed in shallow water and on wet areas, moving very slowly as they take food from the ooze in their slim, grey bills. When not feeding, they may loaf on the shore or swim in sizeable flocks, often mixed with other species.

Male ▼
Tends to look dark with a yellowish patch near tail and a horizontal white stripe

Female ▼
Small, darkish, nondescript; grey bill; face often pale below darker cap

▼ **Flight shape**
Neat, narrow-winged, quite
long-necked, but short-tailed

▼ **Female**
Green hindwing patch with
wide white line in front, little
or no white on trailing edge

▼ **Male**
Wide whitish stripe on midwing;
dark head may contrast with
grey body in some lights

▼ **Flying away**
White midwing bar obvious;
green may flash in bright light

▲ **Underside**
Female has paler forewing
band than garganey

MALE

FEMALE

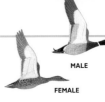

MALE

FEMALE

Mallard
Anas platyrhynchos

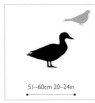

51–60cm 20–24in

DISTRIBUTION
Widespread and generally common by any kind of water; on most coasts in winter

IDENTIFICATION A big, heavy duck, with obvious male and female differences for most of the year. Males from late autumn to spring have a dark green head, white collar, and grey body; in summer they are like darker, redder versions of females, but with curly central tail feathers. Females have dark bodies (no white belly) and white underwings. Purple-blue wing patch with white edges always characteristic. Female has loud, coarse, repeated *quaark quaark quaark*; male makes quiet whistles.

▲ **Up-ending**
Orange legs; white sides to tail; male has black stern

HABITAT All kinds of water and waterside habitats, but not often on open sea; also feeds on fields and marshes away from open water.

BEHAVIOUR Truly wild mallards are handsome, shy wildfowl, but easily become accustomed to people and can be quite tame. Others are crossed with farmyard breeds descended from mallards, and a variety of plumage colours, from all-white to almost black, can be seen in places. Mallards often fly to fields to feed on grain at night.

▼ **Female**
Uniformly brown, streaked dark; often has marked pale stripe over eye; blurred orange and olive bill

▼ **Male**
Pale, with dark hind end, dark head, brownish bands beside back; large size helpful clue

FEMALE

MALE

▼ Flight action
Flight is swift and direct; wings usually beat below body level

▼ Male
Dark inner hindwing patch, with white stripe both in front and behind

▲ Male
Wings whistle in flight; looks long-necked, heavy-bodied, but wings also long and pointed

▲ Female
Big and dark, long in front of wings, but very short behind

Female ►
Large head and bill; bright orange legs; blue wing patch; white tail

▼ Male
Glossy head, chocolate breast, white neck ring; in summer, streaked red-brown with same yellow bill and curly tail feathers

Pintail
Anas acuta

▼ Winter male
Grey and white, with snaky white
neck stripe and vivid white breast;
buff and black by tail

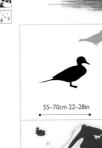

55–70cm 22–28in

DISTRIBUTION
Widespread, but local
in winter, on large
estuaries and floods;
sparse and erratic
breeding bird

IDENTIFICATION A striking duck
in winter, when the males are in full
plumage: the white breast is conspicuous
and the vertical neck stripe unique. The
shoveler has much darker flanks, a blacker
head, and orange legs. Although the
pintail's body is closely barred grey, it can
look very dark at a distance, especially
against gleaming wet mud.

Females and summer males are less
obvious: look for the slender neck, round
head, grey bill, and dark legs. Females
may look pale, greyish, or rich buff-
brown, with a rather plain face, lacking
the stripes through and over the eye of a
female mallard. In flight the long, pointed

Female ►
Pale head, grey bill, sharp tail, grey legs

Male ▼
Neck stripe, white
chest, dark legs

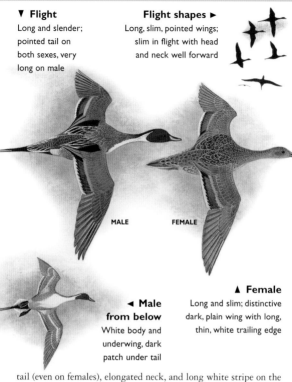

▼ Flight
Long and slender; pointed tail on both sexes, very long on male

Flight shapes ►
Long, slim, pointed wings; slim in flight with head and neck well forward

MALE

FEMALE

◄ Male from below
White body and underwing, dark patch under tail

▲ Female
Long and slim; distinctive dark, plain wing with long, thin, white trailing edge

tail (even on females), elongated neck, and long white stripe on the trailing edge of the wing are obvious. It is a quiet bird: the female has a low, subdued quack.

HABITAT Pintails like flooded marshes and pastures, saltmarsh with sheltered creeks and short, green swards, and open mudflats in wide estuaries. They appear on inland waters in small numbers.

BEHAVIOUR A wild and rather shy duck, not easy to approach closely. It is very local in distribution and often found rather sporadically in ones and twos, but in favoured places gathers in hundreds. It frequently loafs around doing very little by day and feeds at dawn and dusk, but also feeds quietly on weed-covered mud or in shallow floods. It forms less dense flocks than the wigeon, although in flight may pack into coordinated groups or string out in long lines and V-shapes.

Loafing ▼
Often stands on dry ground; short-legged, quite full-bodied shape

Shoveler
Anas clypeata

▼ Male in winter
Green-black head, yellow eye;
bright white breast contrasts
with dark rufous body

44–52cm 17–20in

DISTRIBUTION
Widespread, but
quite localized
and mostly
scarce; small
concentrations
on estuaries and
lakes in winter

IDENTIFICATION The striking male in breeding plumage (late autumn to late spring) is obvious, but in summer it looks more like a dark, very red-brown female, often with a darker head marked with a broad, white facial crescent. Females are broad-bodied ducks that swim low in the water, shoulders almost awash when feeding, but most easily identified in flight. Male has low whistles; female a harsh, loud quack. In flight, wings make a muffled "whoofing" noise.

HABITAT Shallow lakes, floods, saltmarsh creeks, overgrown marshland edges; also quiet, muddy estuaries.

BEHAVIOUR A quiet bird, social where it is common, sometimes feeding in tight, swirling groups, but usually pottering about in shallow water or on mud, where it uses its large bill to sieve food from the water and ooze. It is relatively tame and less highly strung than other ducks.

◄ Female
Underside dark, like
mallard, without white
belly of wigeon, gadwall

◄ Male in flight
Large dark head and bill,
broad white foreparts,
dark underside, pale
blue forewings

◄ Female
Dark body,
elongated head and
bill; grey-blue
forewing patch
distinctive

FEMALE

▲ Males ►
Three-tone pattern from
below distinctive; other
ducks with dark head and
white breast do not have
dark underbody

◄ Young female
Shape and basic pattern
as adult female; pale
forewing duller;
darker, more
blotched body

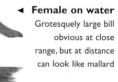

◄ Female on water
Grotesquely large bill
obvious at close
range, but at distance
can look like mallard

Tufted Duck
Aythya fuligula

Summer female ▶
Rich, dark chocolate
brown with variable white
face patch and small tuft;
bill has broad black tip

40–47cm 16–18in

DISTRIBUTION
Widespread, often
abundant on
sheltered coasts,
lakes, and reservoirs
in winter; local in
summer

IDENTIFICATION A diving duck, which slips under from the
surface to feed. Males from autumn to spring are sharply black and
white, with white flanks and loose head tuft; in summer they become
dark brown. Females are brown and usually obviously darker, more
uniform than pochards, but sometimes recall the larger, white-faced
female scaup. Both sexes have a long, white wing stripe at all times.

HABITAT Essentially freshwater, including coastal lagoons, gravel
pits, reservoirs, and lakes of all kinds, not so often on open sea, but in
huge numbers in the brackish waters of the Low Country coasts.

▼ **Males**
Black and white; long
tuft; browner in
summer, retaining tuft

▼ **Females**
Dark overall; may have
white on face, but rarely
so much as scaup; bill looks
small; bright yellow eye

◀ **Female**
Some are white
under tail, like
ferruginous duck

▼ Bills compared
Scaup (head-on and broad bill) has black "nail" on bill tip, blurred on juvenile; tufted (right) has narrow bill with more black

TUFTED

SCAUP

▲ Compare with scaup
Tufted (top) has black band on bill tip and narrow bill; typically less white than shown; head tuft

◄ ▲ Scaup
Scaup has bigger head with no trace of tuft; usually much more white; pale ear patch in summer

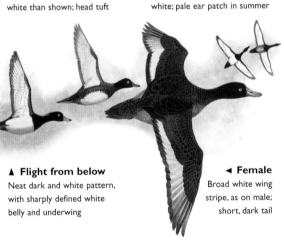

▲ Flight from below
Neat dark and white pattern, with sharply defined white belly and underwing

◄ Female
Broad white wing stripe, as on male; short, dark tail

BEHAVIOUR Usually in flocks, from a few dozen to many thousands strong, often mixed with pochards: in the IJsselmeer, the shores may be fringed with tens of thousands of ducks, mostly these two species. Tufted ducks feed by day (pochards often at night), diving frequently, but spend hours resting, half asleep, in sheltered bays.

Female in winter ►
Often on shore; grey legs and squat, upright form; tuft may be hidden

Scaup
Aythya marila

IDENTIFICATION Similar to black-backed tufted duck and grey-bodied pochard, male scaup has handsome and distinctive combination of black head, grey back, and white flanks. Female less easy, but bigger than tufted duck, with bolder face pattern. Juveniles less distinct, with blurred face and bill patterns, but their slightly larger size, wider body, and rounder head help pick them out from tufted ducks.

HABITAT The marine equivalent of the tufted duck and pochard, preferring much more open water, but also quiet estuaries and bays. It is generally scarce, but regular, on inland lakes and reservoirs.

BEHAVIOUR In summer, breeding

42–51cm 17–20in

DISTRIBUTION
Rare breeder in Europe; in winter, widespread but localized on coasts, numerous in regular favoured areas

▲ **Female below**
White underwing and white belly; quite large, heavy bird, bulkier and longer than tufted

▲ **Female above**
Wide white wing bar recalls tufted duck; facial blaze may be visible in flight; heavier than tufted

Male in flight ►
Long-necked, grey, white, and black duck, with pale back (unlike tufted) and wide wing bar; white body from below

▼ Female
Broader beam than tufted; round head never shows trace of tuft; gleaming yellow eye; white facial blaze eyecatching

▼ On water
Male black both ends, pale in middle; black head and white flanks unlike pochard, grey back unlike tufted

MALE

FEMALE

scaup occur on isolated lakes in the north, often one or two pairs in otherwise quite empty areas, but in Iceland they commonly breed in loose colonies. In winter they gather in flocks in favoured areas, over shallows where they can find plenty of molluscs and other small marine creatures. They dive under from the surface to feed out of sight underwater. Scaup often mix with other diving ducks such as scoters and eiders, and come inshore to mix with tufted ducks and pochards in places. Usually these are ones and twos, mixed with larger numbers of the commoner birds.

JUVENILE

SUMMER FEMALE

Head and bill patterns ►
Pale ear patch distinguishes from tufted duck; smooth, sweeping head profile with no tuft; small, blurred face patch on juvenile matched by some tufteds

Eider
Somateria mollissima

▼ Males in flight
Large, heavy but fast-flying; striking patterns of black-and-white

▲ Females
Direct flight is low, heavy, but swift and powerful; dark, uniform, broad-winged, and long-headed

Male ▶
Note white breast and black belly; similar shoveler has dark head

50–70cm 20–28in

DISTRIBUTION
Widespread all year, many isolated southern groups well south of breeding range

▼ Breeding male
Immaculate from late autumn to spring, with black cap, green nape patches, pale to deep pink breast, white back, black belly

▼ Female standing
Dark, barred, heavy-bodied, short-legged; bill and legs dull greyish, no bright colours

Eclipse males ▲
Patchy in summer, often white on breast, white patch near tail

IDENTIFICATION

Long facial "wedge" beside deep, triangular bill gives a characteristic profile. Males in breeding plumage unmistakable, but young males and summer males are patchy and variable.

◄ Female
Big, brown duck with weak pattern; dark hindwing with no white trailing edge, but narrow white line on midwing

HABITAT Low-lying rocky shores and islands, nesting among low vegetation, shingle, and boulders. At other times on open sea, sheltered bays, and estuaries.

BEHAVIOUR Breeds in small groups, ducklings often gathering in creches for defence against predatory gulls. Otherwise usually in flocks, from a dozen to many thousands strong, diving for food in shallow water over mussel beds and rocky outcrops.

Juvenile ▼
Pale stripe over eye

▼ On water
Wide-bodied; wedge-shaped head; tail often cocked when resting

Long-tailed Duck
Clangula hyemalis

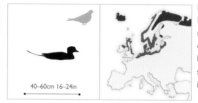

40–60cm 16–24in

DISTRIBUTION
Local breeder in far
north; in winter
quite widespread
but local, except for
scattered isolated
individuals

▼ **Males**
Summer (left) very dark, with
pale facial disk, white flanks;
winter (right) pale with dark
cheek and breastband;
pink band on bill

▼ **Males**
Long, whippy tail; white
flank and under tail; pink
on bill; white or greyish
face in summer

SUMMER

Males ►
Buoyant
on rough
sea; patterns
can be confusing

WINTER

Juvenile ▼
Dark grey bill; dark cheek;
white around eye

▲ **Females**
Dark cap and cheek in summer
(top two), much whiter in winter
(lower two), but juvenile darker-
faced with broad cheek patch

▲ **Young male**
Like female, but
pink on bill

▼ Female in flight
Dark upperside, plain wings, and white sides to black-centred rump recall guillemot, but longer wings and blunter head

▼ Male in flight
Fast-moving dark wings and much white on head and body give dazzling piebald effect

◄ Female
Short, dumpy duck with dark wings, may be puzzling unless head pattern is seen

Flight ▲
Long-tailed male obvious; wings dark above and below

IDENTIFICATION The varied and striking patterns of this small, sea-going duck give distinctive characters, yet they can be difficult to grasp in a brief view. The plain, dark upperwing on a bird showing much white is a useful clue in flight. Juvenile and female birds, which often turn up in isolation outside the main winter range, typically have dark crowns and dark cheeks surrounded by whitish lines. Short, stubby bill, with pink band on males.

HABITAT Shallow seas; the wide, sandy mouths of estuaries and sandy bays are favoured, but long-tailed ducks may be seen on almost any kind of coast. Odd birds turn up in winter in harbours, estuaries, on coastal lagoons, and on reservoirs inland.

BEHAVIOUR A lively and attractive duck, often in large flocks. It delights in noisy displays, with far-carrying *aar-aar-ardl-ow* calls from groups of males showing off to females. It rides out storms quite easily, often mixed with scoters, well offshore, and can be seen flying low over the sea in ones and twos, or long lines of several dozen birds, frequently moving around to find new feeding areas.

Common Scoter
Melanitta nigra

45–55cm 18–22in

DISTRIBUTION
Local breeder, scarce except in far north; widespread in winter, but great majority occur in a few favoured, traditional areas

IDENTIFICATION   Wide-bodied, large-headed diving duck, with thin, waisted neck, often obvious when the head is raised, and a characteristic pointed tail. Males all black, except for yellow patch on top of the bill. Females have pale faces, recalling red-crested pochard, but are otherwise much darker and plain-winged.

HABITAT   Breeds beside remote northern pools in moorland and tundra. Flocks occur farther south all year, in thousands from late summer to spring in wide, open bays. Small numbers regular inland.

▼ **Winter male**
All black above; paler beneath wingtip when seen from below, or flapping on sea

▼ **Winter female**
All dark above (velvet scoter has white hindwing)

◀ **Wingtip**
Narrow outer feather creates whistling sound in flight

▼ Female
Heavy, dark body, extended head on narrow neck, pale face; obvious pale underwing

▼ Young female
Blotchy pale belly, whitish face, pale underwing; all look long-necked, heavy-bodied, quite broad-winged in flight

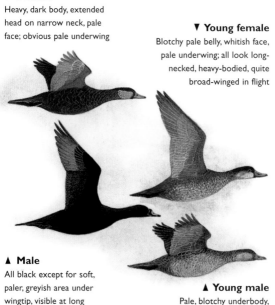

▲ Male
All black except for soft, paler, greyish area under wingtip, visible at long range; slender neck

▲ Young male
Pale, blotchy underbody, darker wingtips

BEHAVIOUR This sea-going diving duck rides out winter storms in very large, tightly packed flocks, which periodically appear and disappear on the rolling swell far offshore. Groups break off and fly away in lines or packs, low over the waves. They display frequently, with raised heads and tails, and far-carrying, whistling calls.

▼ On water
Female dark with paler cheeks, less clear in summer; male black with yellow on bill; pointed tail often cocked

▼ Summer male
Black extensively obscured by brown; yellow bill patch

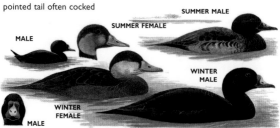

SUMMER MALE

SUMMER FEMALE

MALE

WINTER MALE

WINTER FEMALE

MALE

Velvet Scoter
Melanitta fusca

◄ Female
Dark underbody, pale underwing, white hindwing

▲ Male
All black except for paler underwing, white hindwing panel

◄ Young male
Like blackish female, but white belly

52–59cm 21–23in

DISTRIBUTION
Breeds in far north, local; occurs in non-breeding areas most of year, but mainly autumn to spring, local on coasts

IDENTIFICATION Flocks of velvet scoters are easy to identify, but the usual problem is picking out a few in a large common scoter flock, often at long range, or identifying an isolated bird away from its usual range. At long range this is difficult unless one flaps its wings or takes flight, when the white wing panel is instantly obvious. Otherwise the male's bill and face pattern is unique if seen well; the female's double face patches are distinctive. The characteristic red legs may be seen occasionally. It is a bulky, eider-like scoter, but shares the typical scoter thin neck and pointed tail, which add a shapely quality to this sea-going diving duck.

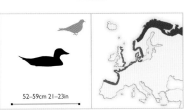

HABITAT Breeds beside northern lakes. Non-breeders in summer and wintering birds are often well offshore in open sea, in large, shallow bays,

▲ Wing flap
White shows at great range when bird rises in water to flap wings

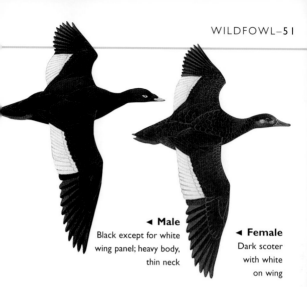

◄ Male
Black except for white
wing panel; heavy body,
thin neck

◄ Female
Dark scoter
with white
on wing

occasionally estuaries, often with common scoters. Occasional
individuals turn up inland, on lakes and reservoirs.

BEHAVIOUR   Scoters are all expert swimmers, at home on the
open sea, frequently hidden from shore by a big swell or choppy
surface. Velvet scoters mix with common scoters and eiders, feeding
by diving underwater for long periods and periodically moving to a
new area in low, fast flights over the sea. They are lively birds, diving
for mussels, cockles, crabs, and starfish, or displaying with raised
heads and cocked tails, often sitting up in the water with a hurried
flap of the wings.

Juvenile ►
Dark face with obscure pale
area; dark bill; long face/bill
profile useful

Female ▼
Double pale face spots, fade to
white; wedge-shaped head;
white on wing may not show

Male ▼
Complex bill pattern;
white around eye
visible at close
range; pointed tail

Goldeneye
Bucephala clangula

42–50cm 17–20in

DISTRIBUTION
Breeds widely but locally in N Europe; widespread inland and on coasts from September to April

IDENTIFICATION Stocky, diving frequently or swimming asleep with cocked tail; looks round-backed with tapered tail, high-peaked head and triangular bill. Male obvious; female often very dark on water, with white collar inconspicuous (absent on immature), but white on wing often shows as horizontal patch. Yellow on bill variable. Wings whistle loudly in fast, direct flight.

HABITAT Breeds beside northern lakes with wooded banks or islands; in winter on lakes, reservoirs, sheltered coasts.

BEHAVIOUR Often inconspicuous because it dives so often. More than expected may appear when disturbed, flying off low and fast. Gathers in flocks to rest. Displays with head-bobbing actions.

Female ▼
Dark head and body, white collar; deep, dark bill; round-shouldered shape

▼ Male
Strikingly white, with black back, black head with big white face spot; large white wing patches in flight

IMMATURE

FEMALE

MALE

FEMALE

Smew
Mergus albellus

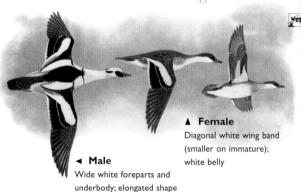

▲ **Female**
Diagonal white wing band
(smaller on immature);
white belly

◄ **Male**
Wide white foreparts and
underbody; elongated shape

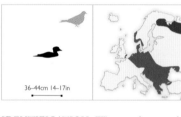

36–44cm 14–17in

DISTRIBUTION
Local breeder in NE
Europe; in winter
on North Sea
coasts and nearby
pools, locally in E
Europe

IDENTIFICATION Winter male eyecatching white with small black marks and grey flanks; in summer more like female. Females and immatures have dark cap with slight crest, clear white lower face (much whiter, smaller cheeks than red-crested pochard or common scoter). Immature males gain white during the winter.

HABITAT Mostly freshwater, including coastal lagoons and pits, but large numbers around Low Country coasts in winter.

BEHAVIOUR Dives frequently; can be inconspicuous, but flocks are lively and social, diving and flying together.

▼ **Winter**
Male white with black face
spot, drooped crest; adult
female has black face,
immature has brown

Red-breasted Merganser
Mergus serrator

◄ **Male in flight**
Long and slim; dark head, dark breastband unlike goosander, white belly

51–62cm 20–24in

DISTRIBUTION
Local breeder, commonest in north; on many coasts in winter, scarce in south

IDENTIFICATION There are three "sawbill" ducks: smew, goosander, and red-breasted merganser. All are diving ducks with narrow bills, serrated on the edges of each mandible. Only the male merganser has a dark breastband; the female is brownest, with the most blurred face and neck pattern. Superficially mallard-like, the male merganser is more sharp-faced, shows much more white, is much more highly strung, and dives frequently. In flight the sawbills have a distinctive shape, with a long tail balancing the long, outstretched head and neck.

HABITAT Breeds close to sea or northern lakes. Outside the breeding season it is a marine bird of open bays and estuaries, or off low-lying rocky coasts.

BEHAVIOUR Mergansers are often seen standing on the shore, in a horizontal pose, on short, red legs, but they are mostly aquatic birds, revelling in the tide race and clean inshore waters. They are usually found in groups, from family parties to flocks up to several hundred strong, often strung out in long lines parallel with the shore. Smaller parties scatter around large estuaries and move with the tides, or fly to and fro between bouts of feeding. Males often display to females, raising their heads and fanning their crests.

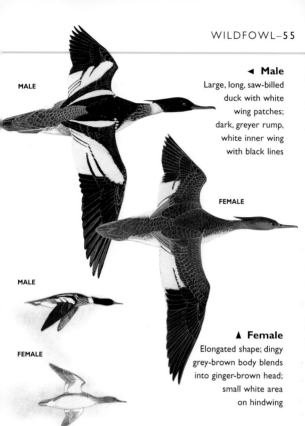

MALE

MALE

FEMALE

MALE

FEMALE

◄ Male
Large, long, saw-billed
duck with white
wing patches;
dark, greyer rump,
white inner wing
with black lines

▲ Female
Elongated shape; dingy
grey-brown body blends
into ginger-brown head;
small white area
on hindwing

▼ Female
Compare face with goosander (left):
slimmer bill, blurry whitish chin (not
clear-cut), no white collar; brownish-
grey body (goosander blue-grey)

▼ Male
Green-black head with wispy
or spiky crest and red spike-
bill (unlike mallard); wide
white collar, mottled breast;
like female in summer, but
more white on wing

GOOSANDER

Goosander
Mergus merganser

Males in flight ▲
Clear white underbody and
neck; inner wing unbroken
white; black wingtips

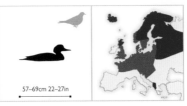

57–69cm 22–27in

DISTRIBUTION
Breeds beside lakes
and rivers; in winter
on lakes, reservoirs,
some sheltered
coasts

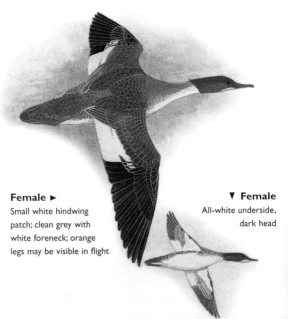

Female ►
Small white hindwing
patch; clean grey with
white foreneck; orange
legs may be visible in flight

▼ Female
All-white underside,
dark head

Winter pair ►
Immaculate from late autumn to late spring; male drab in summer

Winter ▼
Female (upper) clean bluish-grey; white breast and white chin sharply defined; shaggy crest. Male whitish to deep salmon-pink; deep red bill

▼ Male and female
Large, long- and heavy-bodied, with drooped crest and deep-based, hooked bill

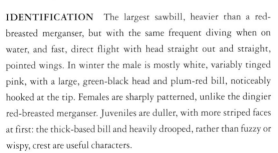

IDENTIFICATION The largest sawbill, heavier than a red-breasted merganser, but with the same frequent diving when on water, and fast, direct flight with head straight out and straight, pointed wings. In winter the male is mostly white, variably tinged pink, with a large, green-black head and plum-red bill, noticeably hooked at the tip. Females are sharply patterned, unlike the dingier red-breasted merganser. Juveniles are duller, with more striped faces at first: the thick-based bill and heavily drooped, rather than fuzzy or wispy, crest are useful characters.

HABITAT Less marine than the merganser, goosanders nest beside rivers and lakes, in holes in trees. In summer they feed on fast-flowing rivers; in winter, they are mostly on freshwater lakes, but some large flocks can be seen on sheltered coasts around the Low Countries and in the Baltic.

BEHAVIOUR Goosanders form small flocks on inland lakes in winter, and larger ones on some coasts. They are a little less prone to displaying, fighting, and flying around than the more energetic mergansers and smews.

Red-throated Diver
Gavia stellata

▼ Compare with black-throat
Black-throated (top) has darker cap to eye; straighter, darker-tipped bill than red-throated (below)

◄ Winter
White extends above eye and almost meets on nape; pale-streaked cap

50–60cm 20–24in

DISTRIBUTION
Scarce and local breeding bird; widespread, but mostly scarce on coasts in winter

IDENTIFICATION Although the smallest diver, it can look big when swimming offshore. Characteristically holds its head uptilted, showing bill slightly upcurved on lower edge. Never has white chequers above, but has fine white speckling in winter. Dark red throat in summer, white face extending above eye in winter. In flight it is quicker, with whippier wingbeats, than the other divers, and its trailing legs are not so long and heavy. In summer it gives wailing and cackling calls, and loud, staccato quack in flight.

HABITAT Breeds on small moorland and tundra pools, flying to the sea to feed. In winter mostly on the sea, on open coasts, but drifting into estuaries with the rising tide; rare inland.

BEHAVIOUR Often solitary, it may gather in loose groups of tens, rarely 100 or more, offshore in winter. Dives underwater for lengthy periods to feed.

◄ Upperparts
White spots on feather edges, unlike other divers

◄ Flight
Slightly drooped, thin neck gives more hunchbacked appearance than other divers; quicker, deeper wingbeats

▲ From below
Straight-line head, body, and trailing legs; extensive white underside and underwing

◄ From above
Dark, greyish but white face often conspicuous; trailing feet look relatively small

▲ Flight
Quite fast, with deep wingbeats, upbeat well above body level

Summer ▼
All-dark back; grey head striped on nape; red throat narrow at top, may look very dark; uptilted bill

▼ Winter adult
White face more extensive than on other divers; speckled with white above

▼ Juvenile
Head largely grey; rely on bill shape, speckled back

Black-throated Diver
Gavia arctica

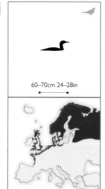

60–70cm 24–28in

DISTRIBUTION
Rare breeder on
northern lakes; in winter
widely but very thinly
spread around coasts,
rare inland

IDENTIFICATION A medium-large diver, not always obviously bigger than a red-throated, but usually noticeably slighter than the great northern. In summer, its chequered back and grey head are diagnostic; in winter it is harder to identify, but the straight bill, lack of obvious dark collar at base of neck, and clear white flank patch are helpful. Immatures in winter have pale scaly feather edges above, compared with the broader, squarer bands on great northerns and white speckles on red-throated divers.

HABITAT Large lakes with small islands in summer; in winter, open coasts of all kinds, estuary mouths, sandy bays.

BEHAVIOUR Pairs frequent breeding lakes in summer, but soon gather in small groups on the sea, still in breeding plumage, before dispersing along the coasts farther south in winter. They dive expertly to find fish, slipping under without a ripple and remaining out of sight for a minute or more. They tend to dive or swim off if disturbed, rather than taking flight.

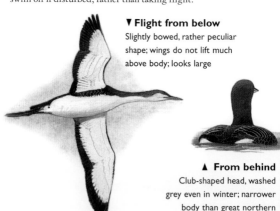

▼ Flight from below
Slightly bowed, rather peculiar
shape; wings do not lift much
above body; looks large

▲ From behind
Club-shaped head, washed
grey even in winter; narrower
body than great northern

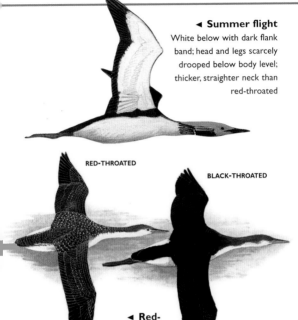

◄ Summer flight
White below with dark flank band; head and legs scarcely drooped below body level; thicker, straighter neck than red-throated

RED-THROATED

BLACK-THROATED

◄ Red-throated
Smaller, slimmer, paler, white-faced

◄ Winter
All dark above, blackest winter diver on back and rump; large feet

▼ Summer
Grey head blends into blacker chin; wide black throat; small white breast patch; chequered ovals on back

WINTER

▲ Winter
Blackish back, greyer nape; dark "notch" into white cheek; small but obvious white flank patch

▲ Juvenile
Greyish; straight bill; grey "notch" into whiter cheek; white flank patch

Great Northern Diver
Gavia immer

73–88cm 29–35in

DISTRIBUTION
Rare breeder; in winter, widespread around coasts, but generally scarce, often on open sea; rare inland

IDENTIFICATION Of the three regular divers in Europe, this is the biggest, but the rare white-billed diver is similar in size and general appearance. The black head and chequered back distinguish them from black-throated in summer; in winter the dark flank, dark half collar, and broader body help. The great northern has a long, deep-based bill, held straight (helping to separate it at a distance from the similarly sized immature cormorant), while the white-billed has a pale-tipped bill, angular on its lower edge, which is often tilted upwards. In flight, a great northern diver is a big, long-winged, very impressive bird.

HABITAT Breeds on remote northern pools. Some immatures, and occasional adults in full breeding plumage, remain well south in summer. In winter occurs on all kinds of coasts, including estuaries and in deep water well offshore.

BEHAVIOUR An excellent diver, sliding under from the surface to fish, perhaps emerging several hundred metres away a minute or two later. In winter, usually alone or in pairs, it is easy to overlook in rough, dark sea, but a big, obvious bird on calm water, perhaps at the mouth of an estuary. It is usually silent away from its breeding lakes, where it has a variety of loud wailing and howling calls, but sometimes a wail or series of laughing notes may be heard.

Summer ▼
Black bill, black head, striped collar, and chequered back

Immature ▲
Broad pale bars above, less scaled than black-throated; dark collar; dark flank

▼ Flight, winter

Great northern large, with big feet and
heavy bill; white-billed diver even
heavier, with broader wings, longer feet

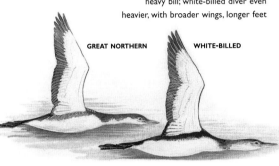

GREAT NORTHERN   **WHITE-BILLED**

◄ Compare with white-billed

In winter, much rarer white-billed has
pale bill without dark ridge; whitish
around eye, paler areas on rear cheeks

Winter ▼

Dark-tipped bill, dark head and
nape, paler back, hint
of darker collar at
base of neck

**WHITE-BILLED
IMMATURE**

Great Crested Grebe
Podiceps cristatus

Flight ▶
Looks hurried and
uncomfortable, with neck
and legs extended and
drooped; big white wing
patches distinctive

DISTRIBUTION
Widespread
breeder inland; in
winter many move
to coasts, especially
estuaries

46–50cm 18–20in

IDENTIFICATION Grebes are much smaller than divers and have different proportions, looking dumpier, rounder-bodied, and longer-necked. The great crested is much larger than all but the red-necked, from which it is separated by its gleaming white breast. In summer its facial adornments are unique; in winter it is longer-necked and more snaky-looking than other grebes. It has loud, harsh growling and barking calls in summer, but is quiet in winter.

HABITAT Breeds on reedy pools, around the edges of reservoirs among flooded willows, and on larger rivers. In winter most move to larger, open reservoirs free from ice, but many can be seen on the

On water ▼
May look larger than it really is; neck
held upright or withdrawn

Winter ▼
Dull, dark body; shiny white
neck and breast striking

Summer ▼
Unique black crest and chestnut
facial frills, erected in display; flat
crown, sharp bill, long, white
neck; more or less rufous along
sides of breast and flanks

Winter ▼
Gleaming white face, neck and breast;
pale stripe above and black line
through eye

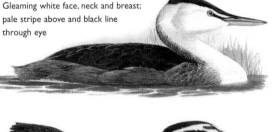

▲ Winter
Dagger bill; pale
stripe over eye,
unlike red-necked

▲ Juvenile
Grey-brown with black-
and-white striped head;
loud, whistling calls

coast from autumn to spring, usually on quiet, inshore waters or in
sheltered estuaries, drifting in and out with the tide.

BEHAVIOUR Even in the breeding season, great crested grebes
are quite social birds, often nesting in loose colonies where
conditions are good. In winter, on reservoirs, flocks may number
scores or even hundreds of birds, but on the sea it is usually seen in
small groups. It is not a frequent flier, and usually flies low over the
water for short distances before splashing back down. It is an expert
swimmer and diver. Like other grebes it is practically unable to walk
on land, although very rarely may be seen standing upright in an
awkward pose on a bank or on its semi-floating nest.

Red-necked Grebe
Podiceps grisegena

▲ **Winter**
Dark cap, no white stripe above eye; yellow on base of bill; pale face defined against dusky neck

▲ **Immature**
Often has more yellow on bill, yellow eye. Face may be dead white, dull, pale grey, or quite dusky, smoky grey

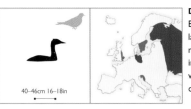

40–46cm 16–18in

DISTRIBUTION
Breeds on reedy lakes and rivers, mostly in E Europe; in autumn and winter, local on coasts

IDENTIFICATION This rather large, rounded grebe is easily identified in summer, but more difficult in winter. At a distance it can be confused with the smaller black-necked and Slavonian grebes (especially dusky-necked moulting or immature birds), or with the larger, slender-necked great crested grebe. It is thicker-set than any of these, with a large, round head and thick bill giving a front-heavy appearance. If the yellow on the bill can be seen, it is diagnostic; the dark breast is also helpful. Winter birds may look dull and dingy, with little of the sparkling white of a great crested or Slavonian, but they do not have the thin, uptilted bill of a black-necked grebe.

HABITAT Red-necked grebes breed on freshwater where there is plenty of waterside vegetation, such as broad rivers and channels

▼ On water
In winter has dull greyish neck, plain white or pale grey face; in summer has rusty neck and breast

WINTER

SUMMER

overhung by willows and tall reeds in the Danube delta. In autumn they gather on quiet coasts, in sandy bays, or off the mouths of estuaries, and sometimes turn up on lakes inland.

BEHAVIOUR Like other grebes, the red-necked dives for its food, catching small fish and aquatic insects of all kinds. It is quite at home on the sea, riding out the swell quite easily, but prefers fairly sheltered water. It may be seen in ones and twos, or small gatherings of up to a dozen, rarely more.

▼ Flight
Like thick-necked great crested, but much less white on wing; long, trailing feet

Juvenile ▼
Striped face, rufous wash on neck

▲ Summer
Black crest can be raised; face whitish to dusky-grey

Slavonian Grebe
Podiceps auritus

Winter ▼
Grey-black above, white below, flanks marble grey; pure white face against black cap; pale spot near eye

Summer ▼
Black head with golden tufts; rufous neck, breast, and flanks

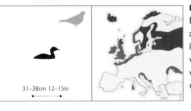

31–38cm 12–15in

DISTRIBUTION
Breeds by northern and northeastern lakes; in autumn and winter disperses widely on coasts, rarely inland

IDENTIFICATION The golden-yellow ear tufts (which fade to a straw colour) and rusty-red neck and breast make this an easy bird to identify in summer, but it is more of a challenge in autumn and winter. Young birds have a hint of rufous on the neck, but winter adults are very black and white, with a sharply defined cap, clean white cheeks that almost meet on the nape, and a bright white foreneck. Black-necked grebes look duskier, often blurred on the edges of the black hindneck and dusky on the foreneck, and have tip-tilted bills. Bigger red-necked grebes are much longer-billed, and also duskier on the foreneck and chest.

SLAVONIAN

BLACK-NECKED

◄ Winter comparison
Slavonian has round or flat head, straight bill with pale tip, pale spot in front of eye; black-necked has uptilted bill, dark ear patch with white "hook"

WINTER ADULT

IMMATURE

Flight ►
Blackish with white on wing; note variable pale spot on inner forewing, unlike black-necked

HABITAT Breeding lakes are often small, open, and exposed, but most successful pairs nest in reeds and rushes in the shallows, where there is more cover from predators and shelter from the wind and waves. In winter, most occur on sheltered coasts, including estuaries, with just a few on pools inland.

BEHAVIOUR Breeding pairs concentrate in small, loose groups on favoured lakes, but in winter Slavonian grebes tend to be less gregarious than black-necked grebes. Often found in ones and twos, sometimes mixed with black-necked and great crested grebes, diving in the shallows and moving around with the tide. The species is an expert diver, but unable to walk on land, and it is not a great flier: it tends to fly low, for short distances, except when on migration. It swims buoyantly, bobbing like a cork, and is a lively, active bird when drifting on a strong current. On quieter waters it is typically more sluggish and subdued.

Black-necked Grebe
Podiceps nigricollis

28–34cm 11–13in

DISTRIBUTION
Widespread but
very local breeder;
equally local in
winter, mostly on
coasts but also
inland

IDENTIFICATION Although one of the smallest grebes, the black-necked can stretch up its neck to look quite large and sleek when alarmed. At other times it looks dumpy. In winter it is dingier than Slavonian, generally with a less crisply defined head pattern (although some can look very alike), an uptilted bill, and a steeper, rounder crown. Winter differences are more evident when the two species are together; single birds can be hard to identify. In summer their plumage patterns are quite different.

HABITAT Breeds on rich lakes with abundant surface and marginal vegetation. In autumn and winter many move to the coast, especially estuaries, and to larger, more open lakes and reservoirs.

BEHAVIOUR As suitable conditions are found in few places, black-necked grebes breed in small groups, occasionally quite large colonies, and they remain social even in winter. A typical winter group contains 10 or 12 birds, perhaps with one or two Slavonian grebes at the fringes. They swim well and dive easily, to find fish and small aquatic creatures underwater. Like other grebes they are not often seen in flight, despite their lengthy migrations.

Immature ►
Like dull winter adult, but hint of rufous on
cheeks, dusky neck

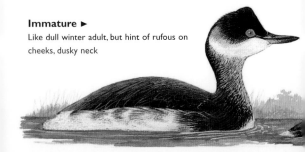

◄ Flight from above
Dark grey and white; note white
hindwing, but no white on
forewing, unlike larger grebes;
legs trail and droop slightly

Winter comparison ▼
Slavonian looks sharper,
black-necked often
duskier, smaller, with
steep forehead

WINTER

BLACK-NECKED

SLAVONIAN

Winter ▼
Steep forehead above tilted bill; black
cap extends onto cheeks, white
hooks up behind cap

Summer ▼
Peaked black head, black
neck and breast; rufous
confined to flanks;
drooped yellow ear
tufts fan out

▲ Winter
Slavonian (left) with
four black-necked;
note variable
pattern

Little Grebe
Tachybaptus ruficollis

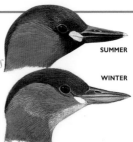

SUMMER

WINTER

Head and bill ►
Round head, thick straight bill;
distinctive yellowish or white
spot at base of bill

23–29cm 9–11in

DISTRIBUTION
Common over
most of southern
and central Europe;
in winter moves to
lowland lakes and
coasts

IDENTIFICATION   The smallest, brownest, roundest grebe, also the most inconspicuous, but summer colours are obvious and even the most contrasted individual in winter never has a white face. The pale spot near the bill is a useful clue.

HABITAT   Breeds on reedy ponds, pools, lakes, flooded pits, and rivers. In winter, leaves smaller pools for larger lakes, rivers, and coastal waters, but is less often seen on the sea than other grebes.

BEHAVIOUR   Secretive in summer, but betrayed by its high-pitched, whinnying notes. In winter occurs in small groups or singly, often on more open water, but still timid and wary.

▼ Flight
Dull, plain brown, with little
wing contrast; trailing feet

WINTER

▼ Winter
Dark forehead and cap, pale
buff-brown cheeks and
foreneck; white bill
spot; tailless shape

WINTER

Summer ▼
Dark cap and breast, rufous
face and foreneck,
yellowish bill spot

WINTER

Fulmar
Fulmarus glacialis

DISTRIBUTION
Breeds around
North Sea, Irish
Sea, Atlantic coasts;
widespread at sea
in winter, most far
offshore

45–50cm 18–20in

IDENTIFICATION A large petrel, pale grey and white, but otherwise not especially gull-like. It cannot walk, and sits flat on cliff ledges or sails on stiff wings alongside cliffs or low over the sea. The large creamy-white head, grey tail, and grey wingtips are distinctive.

HABITAT Breeds on cliffs, some a little way inland; also on buildings, low earth banks, and walls in north. Otherwise, spends most of its time out at sea, following trawlers.

BEHAVIOUR Pairs occupy broad cliff ledges, greeting each other with loud, raucous, cackling calls. They feed at sea, flying expertly in a wind, or more heavily, with shallow flaps, in calm weather.

DARKER NORTHERN FORMS

UNDERSIDE

▲ **Flight**
Pale grey; upperwing fades
brownish, mottled, with
pale patch behind angle;
grey tail, unlike gulls

▲ **On water**
Large white head with short, thick,
blunt bill; leans forward, tail and
wingtips held quite high

Cory's Shearwater
Calonectris diomedea

45–56cm 18–22in

DISTRIBUTION
Local breeder around
Mediterranean; in
summer and autumn
north to Ireland, more
rarely English Channel

IDENTIFICATION A big, powerful, slow-flying shearwater, rising high above waves in strong winds, but with low, rolling flight in calms. Pale brown and white; head may look darker, but no sharp cap effect. Pale bill with dark tip may be visible against dark water in good light.

HABITAT Breeds on cliffs and rocky islands. Otherwise, open sea.

BEHAVIOUR A characteristic seabird of the Mediterranean and North Atlantic islands. Often seen offshore, moving quite slowly, with bowed wings straight or slightly angled back, flying with long glides, a few slow beats, and a swinging, rolling action low over the waves.

▼ **Flight**
White below; much
bigger than Manx

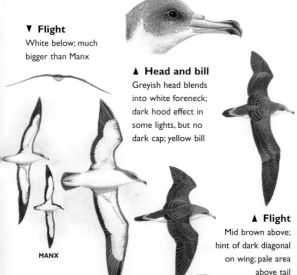

▲ **Head and bill**
Greyish head blends
into white foreneck;
dark hood effect in
some lights, but no
dark cap; yellow bill

MANX

▲ **Flight**
Mid brown above;
hint of dark diagonal
on wing; pale area
above tail

Sooty Shearwater
Puffinus griseus

40–51cm 16–20in

DISTRIBUTION
Appears in North
Sea and North
Atlantic in late
summer and
autumn

IDENTIFICATION Dark, slightly skua-like shearwater, with narrow, angled, pointed wings, and heavy pot belly. All blackish-brown except for variable silvery-white underwing band. Flies with long glides, veering over onto wingtip, and occasional shallow flaps.

HABITAT Breeds in the southern hemisphere, but disperses north in the southern winter. Typical of open sea, but close inshore near headlands at times, especially during periods of onshore winds.

BEHAVIOUR Typical shearwater stiff-winged, gliding flight low over the sea. Usually seen in small numbers, loosely linked in widespread groups or following a line offshore a few at a time. Often occurs in ones and twos with Manx shearwaters.

▼ **Flight**
Dark, with blackish
fading to dull brown;
large body, pointed
head and bill,
long, sharp
wings

◀ **Flight from below**
Banks over to reveal flash of
pale grey or dull white along
underwing

Manx Shearwater
Puffinus puffinus

Flight ►
Blackish above (fades browner
in summer), white below

30–38cm 12–15in

DISTRIBUTION
Breeds locally on
islands, cliffs;
widespread at sea,
but rare in Europe
in winter; rarely
inland after gales

IDENTIFICATION Typically a small, black shape low over the
sea, with stiff, straight wings, veering over to reveal flash of white
underside. Several flickered wingbeats between glides; longer, more
banked glides in strong winds when it may rise high off the water.

HABITAT Breeds in burrows, between rocks, or in scree on islands;
some nest high on remote island hilltops. Otherwise, open sea.

BEHAVIOUR May be seen sitting on the sea, tail-up,
head rather hunched, especially when feeding or
gathering near breeding sites,
but usually seen in flight
over the sea. Comes to
land only to breed and
then only after dark to
avoid predators, with
chorus of wailing and
cackling calls.

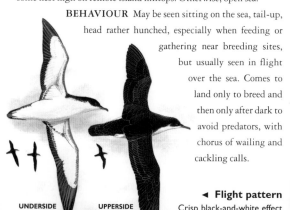

UNDERSIDE   UPPERSIDE

◄ Flight pattern
Crisp black-and-white effect
unless very close; white flank
shows either side of rump

Balearic Shearwater
Puffinus mauretanicus

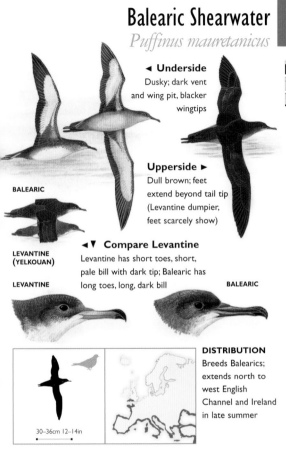

◄ Underside
Dusky; dark vent and wing pit, blacker wingtips

Upperside ►
Dull brown; feet extend beyond tail tip (Levantine dumpier, feet scarcely show)

BALEARIC

LEVANTINE (YELKOUAN)

◄▼ Compare Levantine
Levantine has short toes, short, pale bill with dark tip; Balearic has long toes, long, dark bill

LEVANTINE

BALEARIC

DISTRIBUTION
Breeds Balearics; extends north to west English Channel and Ireland in late summer

30–36cm 12–14in

IDENTIFICATION Mediterranean shearwaters are complex: rare, endangered Balearic is like browner Manx, with dull underside, dark marks under wing. Eastern Mediterranean species (or form), Levantine or Yelkouan shearwater, is commoner. Smaller, paler than sooty shearwater, without big body, narrow wing effect.

HABITAT Breeds on rocky islands; feeds over sea, often north to English Channel, and migrates into Atlantic after breeding season.

BEHAVIOUR Typical shearwater, coming to land only to nest and visiting nests only after dark (or remaining hidden inside burrow all day). Commoner eastern Mediterranean species often seen in long flocks sitting offshore, or flying fast and low.

Storm Petrel
Hydrobates pelagicus

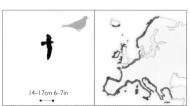

14–17cm 6–7in

DISTRIBUTION
Local nester on cliffs and islands; widespread at sea, rarely seen from most shores

Flight ▶
Wings all dark and slightly rounded; tail round at tip; bold white rump wraps around sides; white underwing stripe; dips to water with lowered feet when feeding

IDENTIFICATION Almost insect-like in minute scale over open sea. Flies quite fast, steadily flapping with swallow-like beats, feeding with bat-like flutter. Broad white rump, round tail, white line beneath wing.

▲ Flight shapes
Wings held out or swept back, broad-based, tapered back to blunt point

HABITAT Nests in holes among rocks on islands; otherwise, occurs only at sea; best seen from ships, occasionally from headlands.

BEHAVIOUR Comes to land only after dark, or remains hidden in burrow. At sea often follows ships, tilting and pattering across wake, but also seen flying alongside or ignoring vessels, travelling at surprising speed. Gathers in small groups where food is available.

Leach's Storm Petrel
Oceanodroma leucorhoa

◄ Impressions
Small petrel, angled wings and active, erratic flight; notched tail; narrow white rump patch

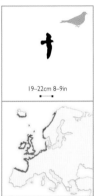

19–22cm 8–9in

Flight shapes ▲
Wings angled, held above body and kinked; tail notched; pale band on upperwing, all dark underwing

DISTRIBUTION
Breeds on a handful of northern islands; widespread at sea in autumn, rare inshore except during gales

IDENTIFICATION A small bird, but markedly larger than storm petrel; wings angled back and kinked up at joint. Tail fork hard to see, but pale wing band clear at moderate range. Rump looks dull white or narrow, with darker central mark. Flight erratic, leaping, bounding; often turning back to spiral down to surface.

HABITAT Nests in burrows on remote islands; at other times, over open sea. Rarely, but much more regularly than storm petrel, blown inland by autumn gales, appearing over larger reservoirs.

BEHAVIOUR A nocturnal visitor to its breeding sites, but tends to be seen from headlands during migration in localized areas, such as Liverpool Bay and southern Irish Sea. It does not follow ships. Leach's Storm Petrel may join other petrels when feeding.

Gannet
Morus bassana

▼ **Adult**
White with yellow-buff
head, black wingtips

Juvenile ►
Blackish with copious white spots;
becomes piebald brown-black and
white with age

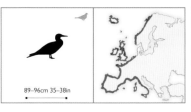

89–96cm 35–38in

DISTRIBUTION
Local breeder
on islands, few
mainland colonies;
widespread at sea,
least common in
winter

IDENTIFICATION A big, impressive seabird. On land, comes to
dense breeding colonies on cliffs, when unmistakable. No other
seabird in Europe is so big and white: its yellowish head, dagger bill,
and short, dark legs make it unique. In flight, strikingly white at
long range, even when most gulls look dull; sharp black wingtips
obvious. Immature has dark back, white head and underside; looks
more like immature gull, but has longer, pointed tail, different wing
shape, and straight-winged, easy, powerful flight.

HABITAT Breeds on large cliff ledges, over rounded tops of rocky
islands, and in a few places on mainland cliffs. Otherwise lives at sea,
but often visible from coasts, sometimes well into large bays.

BEHAVIOUR Gannets breed communally; colonies are noisy,
impressive places, with a constant mechanical-sounding, rhythmic
chorus of deep, throaty, *urrah-urrah* calls. Many displays and postures

are stereotyped and ritualized. At sea, gannets frequently search for fish alone, but where fish are abundant the birds gather in sizeable feeding flocks, plunging in from a height or diving in at an angle from a few metres up. When moving between colonies and fishing areas they often fly steadily, low over the sea, in small groups of up to 10 or so, often line astern. Gannets often pass by headlands in autumn, in small numbers all day long, only loosely connected, but following a regular path just offshore. In strong winds they rise and fall and bank over on one wingtip, like huge shearwaters.

▼ Adult in flight
Long black-tipped wings, extended head and pointed bill longer than pointed tail; regular, shallow wingbeats; soars and glides in wind

Juvenile ▼
Looks greyish, paler under wings; same distinctive shape as adult; much bigger than skuas, but closer to young great black-backed gull

▲ Immature
Over several years, gains more white via several piebald plumages

▲ Fishing
Plunges from height for fish with big splash

Cormorant
Phalacrocorax carbo

SHAG

JUVENILE

SPRING

Flight ▶
Goose-like in flight, with long, straight, round-tipped wings, extended neck, and longish, round tail

▲ On water
Swims very low with tail flat on water, bill uptilted

Adults ▼
Blackish, browner above; white throat patch; in spring, white thigh and whitish head plumes, dark patch near bill

SPRING

WINTER

IMMATURE

90–100cm 35–39in

DISTRIBUTION
Widespread around
most coasts, also
inland, all year
round

IDENTIFICATION A large, dark, broad-backed waterbird with a
thick neck, large flat head, and thick hooked bill. Adult has white
face patch (shag has yellow gape and chin). Immature whiter below
than shag (which has white chin spot), less snaky head, thicker bill.
Heavier flight than shag, often high over land or sea (shag usually
low over waves); capable of soaring at great height. Typically swims
low in water, tail end awash, head up. Holds bill uptilted, unlike
great northern diver.

HABITAT Coastal waters of all kinds, from estuary creeks to open
sea, but usually in sheltered areas such as harbours and river mouths.
Also common inland on lakes and reservoirs.
Nests in colonies on cliffs or in tree tops.

BEHAVIOUR Despite
being very much tied to
water, the cormorant is often seen
loafing around on buoys,
floating platforms, piers,
and harbour walls, as well
as in tall trees beside
inland waters. It feeds
by diving, sliding
or rolling underwater,
without the forward
leap of the smaller shag.

SHAG

IMMATURES

◄ Immatures
Variable amount of white
below, dark brown above;
flattish head with long,
thick bill; upright stance

Shag
Phalacrocorax aristotelis

65–80cm 26–32in

◄ Autumn/ winter
Sleek, oily green-black with delicate dark feather edges; yellow on chin and gape

DISTRIBUTION
Widespread on coasts; different race in Mediterranean; rarely inland after gales

▼ Immature
Upperwing of young bird fades paler across coverts; Mediterranean race has whitish panel

SPRING

IMMATURE

IDENTIFICATION Like a small, dark, slender cormorant. It looks black at any distance, but green at close range with a delicate lacework pattern of black feather edges. Spring adults have a unique upstanding crest, but for most of the year the head is smooth and round, not so flat on the forehead as cormorant, nor so thick-billed. Yellow gape is prominent, but no white chin patch on adults. Immatures dark brown with pale chin, without the white underside of most immature cormorants, but local Mediterranean race does have a white underside except for dark thighs, and marked pale panel across the upperwing.

HABITAT Essentially maritime, breeding on high cliffs with broad ledges and often standing in small parties on rocks near the water. Feeds on open sea or close to rocks, even in surging surf.

BEHAVIOUR Shags fly low over the water in tight groups; cormorants often fly higher, and flocks fly in lines or V-shapes.

JUVENILE

IMMATURE

IMMATURE

MEDITERRANEAN IMMATURE

SUMMER

▲ **Standing**
Immature dark except for pale chin spot, rarely paler chest; later, upperwing fades paler

▲ **Mediterranean**
Mediterranean immature white beneath

When diving to feed, typically makes a forward leap before going under, whereas cormorants usually roll gently out of sight. Very gregarious: while cormorants breed in large colonies in places, and may be seen standing around in sizeable groups, they rarely make such big flocks as shags feeding in the sea, which can number many hundreds. These groups are active and excitable. Often, however, shags stand upright on rocks, motionless for long spells, between feeding bouts. Like cormorants, they stand upright with wings outspread as if to dry them: this may indeed help dry the feathers, but could also assist digestion. Typically shags hold their wings rather more outstretched, straighter than cormorants.

On water ▼
Slim, with rounded, slender head, thin bill; sits low, head uptilted

WINTER

SUMMER

Greater Flamingo
Phoenicopterus ruber

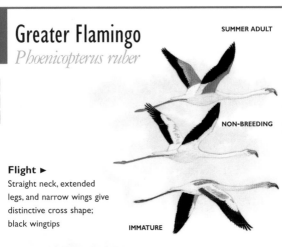

SUMMER ADULT

NON-BREEDING

IMMATURE

Flight ►
Straight neck, extended legs, and narrow wings give distinctive cross shape; black wingtips

◄ Feeding
Hangs head down to toes, bill inverted, to sieve for food in shallows, striding forward slowly

120–145cm 47–57in

DISTRIBUTION
Local breeder and more extensive visitor at all times in Mediterranean region; on marshes, saltpans, lakes

IDENTIFICATION Greater flamingos would be unmistakable in Europe, were it not for occasional escaped Chilean flamingos (which have grey legs and pink "knees") often found outside the greater flamingo's usual range. Flamingos are striking birds, very tall and slim, with elongated legs and necks. They can swim like pale pink swans, and honk rather like geese. In flight the red-and-black wings of birds in breeding plumage catch the eye and are unlike those of any other bird. Flight is direct and quite swift, with regular, shallow beats and occasional glides.

HABITAT Mostly saline lagoons and brackish lakes, usually close to the coast (but farther inland in southern Spain). Breeds on remote

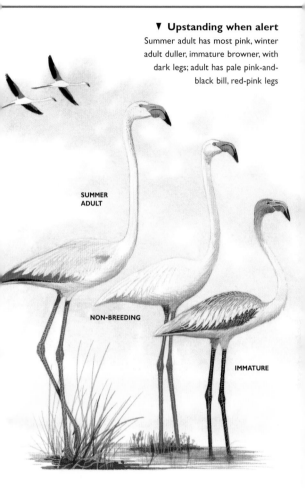

▼ Upstanding when alert
Summer adult has most pink, winter adult duller, immature browner, with dark legs; adult has pale pink-and-black bill, red-pink legs

SUMMER ADULT

NON-BREEDING

IMMATURE

islands and sandbars surrounded by water at a handful of regular European sites; more widespread as non-breeder, even in summer.

BEHAVIOUR Flamingos live in flocks, from a few tens to several thousands strong. They feed in loose or dense groups, gather into tight packs to display, and breed in large, crowded colonies, making low mud mounds for nests. Typically they feed while wading in shallows, their heads down and bills inverted to strain food from the water, but they can wade deeply or swim easily. In flight they make long lines or V-shapes, like geese, settling with legs dangling, wings angled or bowed, and necks curiously bent back in S-shaped curves.

Little Egret
Egretta garzetta

DISTRIBUTION
Widespread in Mediterranean and extending north along Atlantic coast and into North Sea; on estuaries, lakes

55–65cm 22–26in

IDENTIFICATION A neat, compact, white heron, with a thin, often sharply angled neck (may be extended or withdrawn). Yellow feet distinctive. In flight, head sunk into shoulders, feet trailed, wingbeats quicker than grey heron. Occasional harsh calls.

HABITAT Beside lakes, marshes, saline lagoons, and along coasts of all kinds, including both muddy estuaries and rocky shores.

BEHAVIOUR Often feeds using patient "wait and see" strategy; also feeds actively, dancing through shallows or over a marsh, sometimes waving or flapping wings. Nests in tree colonies.

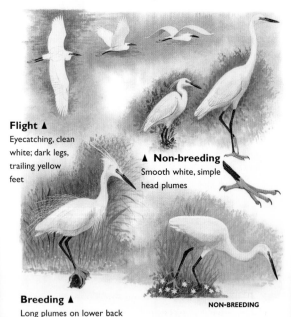

Flight ▲
Eyecatching, clean white; dark legs, trailing yellow feet

▲ Non-breeding
Smooth white, simple head plumes

Breeding ▲
Long plumes on lower back

NON-BREEDING

Great Egret
Ardea alba

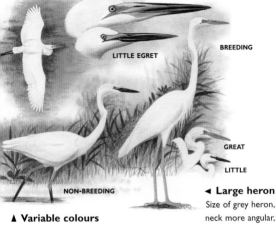

LITTLE EGRET

BREEDING

GREAT

LITTLE

NON-BREEDING

◀ **Large heron**
Size of grey heron,
neck more angular,
all-white except
for bill and legs

▲ **Variable colours**
Bill often all-yellow, blacker in spring;
legs black or with yellow above joint,
or all-yellowish in summer

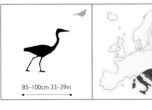

85–100cm 33–39in

DISTRIBUTION
Breeds in E Europe,
very locally in Low
Countries; erratic in
W Europe in all
months on marshes,
coastal lakes

IDENTIFICATION A big egret, at least as tall as grey heron when erect, neck very long and angular, bill heavier than little egret's and yellow for most of year. Legs black, yellow, or combination of the two. In flight, wings broad, bowed; wingbeats slower than little egret's, and long legs trail farther beyond tail.

HABITAT Large swamps, reedbeds, and adjacent flooded fields, sometimes open lakes, fish ponds, flooded pits, low-lying coasts.

BEHAVIOUR More heron-like than the smaller, more active than little egret, often standing immobile for long periods; also perches in trees, especially in summer. May mix with other egrets and herons, particularly where large concentrations of fish attract them, as at artificial fish ponds, making excited feeding flocks.

Grey Heron
Ardea cinerea

90–98cm 35–39in

DISTRIBUTION
Very widespread
all year, but only
in summer in far
north and east;
frequent on all
coasts

IDENTIFICATION A large, upstanding waterside bird, which holds head erect or withdrawn into rounded shoulders. Long, dagger bill, snaky neck, long legs with large feet; in flight has broad, rounded, bowed wings, and slow wingbeats. Grey, paler below and on neck. Adult has white head with black stripe through eye continuing into thin crest; juvenile plainer and greyer, with dark cap. In flight, shows whitish patch towards outer part of forewing, especially in head-on view. Loud, grating *fraank* call.

HABITAT All kinds of water, from pools and rivers to larger reed-fringed and open lakes, saltmarsh, and sheltered coasts, both muddy

▼ Flight
Pale grey with grey-black flight feathers; trailing feet;
arched wings always distinctive; acrobatic over colonies

TREETOP NESTS

▲ Flight shapes
Head withdrawn; wings bowed; legs
trailing; ponderous in direct flight

and with seaweed-covered rocks and rock pools. Nests in tall trees (or, in north, in low bushes, in extensive marshes, or on ground).

BEHAVIOUR A rather slow-moving, patient hunter of fish, frogs, and small rodents on the water's edge, either with a steady, slow-stepping, stalking walk, or by standing still for long periods until prey comes within range. To grasp its prey, uses a sudden dart of the head and neck. Small fish are swallowed immediately, but larger ones, and especially slimy eels (a favourite food), may be carried to drier ground or first washed in clear water, before being killed and swallowed. Grey herons are noisy at the nest, with many harsh croaks, strident cries, and noisy bill-clattering. They are also surprisingly acrobatic in flight over the colony, descending from great heights with swift, twisting dives.

▼ Breeding plumage
In summer has long, pale back plumes, elongated black crest; bill bright, briefly orange or pink

SUMMER

EARLY SPRING

WINTER

JUVENILE

▲ Adult
Grey with black shoulder patch; white head and neck with black stripe behind eye; green-yellow bill

▲ Juvenile
Grey, rather dull and plain; grey head and neck, dark grey cap, dull bill

Honey Buzzard
Pernis apivorus

▼ Flight patterns
Plain above except for dark
bands on tail (two at base) and
trailing edge of wings

Flight ▲
Honey (top) longer-
tailed than common
buzzard (lower)

◄ Tail patterns
Male (left), female
(centre), juvenile (right)

▲ Perched
Small bill; yellow eyes in round
head; rather short, arched claws

▲ Head pattern
Juvenile (left) often whitish, dark
eyes; adult greyer, yellow eyes

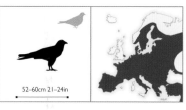

52–60cm 21–24in

DISTRIBUTION
Breeds in woods;
migrates along
coasts and over
shortest sea
crossings, as at
Gibraltar, Malta,
Bosphorus

IDENTIFICATION A large, broad-winged, buzzard-like bird of
prey, usually seen in flight. Compared with common buzzard, shows
a longer, narrower head and a longer tail, often slightly rounded and
broadest in the middle when closed, broad and round when fanned.
Long wings may be angled on leading edge and straight at rear, or
have more of an S-shaped trailing edge. Wings narrow at the body,
with broader, floppier look than common buzzard on bigger females.
Flight typically looks lazier, more relaxed, with deeper, more elastic,
less jerky wingbeats; glides with wings flat or drooped, not raised in
shallow V. Dark tail bands diagnostic if seen well, two or three at base
and one at tip of tail; yellow eye also distinctive at close range.

Flight pattern from beneath ▼
Often dark, with darker wrist (carpal) patch on wing;
dark trailing edge to wing; dark bands at base and tip
of tail separated by gap; variable barring on underparts
and wings (more on female) often striking

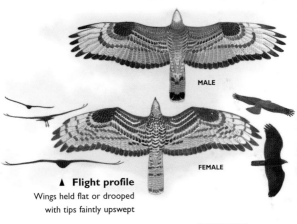

MALE

FEMALE

▲ Flight profile
Wings held flat or drooped
with tips faintly upswept

JUVENILE MALE

Autumn juveniles ▲
Often pale below; may have weak
tail bars, but often strongly
barred beneath body and wings

JUVENILE FEMALE

HABITAT A forest bird, but a migrant to Africa in autumn,
returning in spring, moving in large flocks that circle in rising air
currents or drift along the coast, so may be seen almost anywhere.

BEHAVIOUR Feeds on wasps, bees, their grubs, wax, and honey at
nests in woodland, following flying insects to discover their nests,
which it digs out with its feet. Consequently hard to see in thick
forest except during overhead display flights, but easier on
migration, when it flies in the open, often in large flocks.

Black Kite
Milvus migrans

55–60cm 22–24in

DISTRIBUTION
Widely distributed summer visitor to E, C, and especially S Europe, rare migrant in NW Europe, often in coastal areas

IDENTIFICATION A large, buzzard-like bird of prey with a triangular tail, less deeply notched than red kite's. Looks dark, like female marsh harrier or dark booted eagle, but shows pale diagonal band across upperwing (unlike harrier) and has more angled wings than either, often held up in slight kink at wrist. Active flight relaxed, elastic, elegant, with soft, easy wingbeats; may twist tail as a rudder, more than harriers or booted eagle. Red kite has whiter patch

▲ From below
Dark brown, rather plain wings and tail; greyer head; paler brown body and coverts; juvenile more rufous

▼ Juvenile
Paler, more reddish than adult, with contrasted narrow dark centres to paler feathers, and white tips to longer wing coverts

JUVENILE

under wing; paler, more translucent, more deeply forked tail; even more elegant, light flight action. High, squealing calls.

HABITAT Occurs over all kinds of ground from open heathy places to thicker woodland with clearings, especially near riversides or lakes. Migrates along coasts or across narrowest sea crossings such as Gibraltar and Bosphorus, or over Sicily and Malta, together with other birds of prey and storks.

BEHAVIOUR Hunts over open ground and waterside areas, diving to take prey or dropping to feed on road kills, other dead animals, or refuse of all kinds. Often gathers in small groups around rubbish tips, typically with red kites, Egyptian vultures, and other scavengers. Kites frequently chase other birds, including other birds of prey such as red kites, attempting to steal food.

▼ Flight
Dark, with pale diagonal across upperwing; paler behind bend of wing, especially on more rusty-bodied juvenile; shallow tail fork or notch, triangular with square tip when fanned

ADULT

JUVENILE

ADULT

JUVENILE

◄ Adult
Dark, with slightly paler, greyer head, often dark line through pale eye

RED KITE

Red Kite
Milvus milvus

▲ **Adult and juvenile**
Adult (lower) bright rufous with streaked
grey head, paler wing coverts, pale eye;
juvenile has whiter feather edges, dark eye

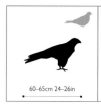

60–65cm 24–26in

DISTRIBUTION
Widespread all year
in S and W Europe,
summer in C and E
Europe, common in
Mediterranean area

IDENTIFICATION Large, long-winged bird of prey, very
flexible and elegant in flight. More rufous than black kite, especially
on tail, with bolder white wing patch. Compared with common
buzzard is longer-winged, much less stiff, does not soar with wings
raised in V. Compared with marsh harrier, wings more bowed, not
raised in stiff V, more rufous than all except adult male harrier which
is distinguished by plain, pale grey on wing and tail. Loud, squealing
call higher, thinner, and longer than buzzard's.

HABITAT Open ground, woodland, marshland, and coastal
lagoons; migrates along the coast.

BEHAVIOUR When looking for food it flies low, steadily, circling
or beating slowly ahead with deep, elastic wingbeats, but twists or
dives down to ground with great speed and agility. Also hunts other
birds with great turn of speed over short distance. Often chases, or is
chased by, black kites and buzzards. Frequently seen perched upright
on telegraph pole or bare branch, or more horizontally on the ground.

▼ Flight from below

Rufous, with blacker wings except for bold white patch behind angle; tail pale, darker at corners of deep fork

BLACK KITE

ADULT

JUVENILE

▲ Compare with black

Black kite a little stockier, darker, duller, less contrasted; underwing has more diffuse, less striking, pale patch

Adult ▲

Paler edges to upperwing feathers create pale diagonal band across inner wing

Flight ►

Distinctive shape, with long, quite narrow, angled wings, small head, and long, notched, or forked tail (more triangular when spread); bold white patch on inner primary feathers, blacker wingtip

Flight profile ►

Both kites have bowed wings; red more extreme, longer-winged shape (booted eagle, honey buzzard have flatter wings)

BLACK

RED

White-tailed Eagle
Haliaeetus albicilla

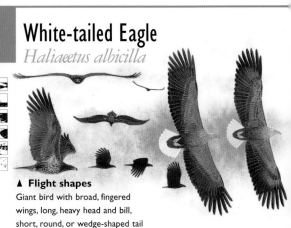

▲ **Flight shapes**
Giant bird with broad, fingered
wings, long, heavy head and bill,
short, round, or wedge-shaped tail

70–92cm 28–36in

DISTRIBUTION
Widespread, but
very local, mostly
rare on marshes,
deltas; in W Europe,
rare winter visitor
mostly to coasts

IDENTIFICATION   A huge eagle,
vulture-like in size, body bulk, breadth of
wing, and short tail length (golden eagle more
elegant, with longer tail). Deep, slow wingbeats
between long glides on flat wings (golden eagle
typically soars with wings held up in V). Adult pale
brown with whitish head, bright white tail, yellow
bill. Immatures darker, more spotted above, pale beneath
with dark streaks, tail dark at first, showing white streaks when
fanned, bill dark-tipped.

HABITAT Large freshwater lakes, marshes,
coastal lagoons, coastal cliffs, islands.

BEHAVIOUR Flies over feeding areas
searching for dead animals, especially fish,
or diving to snatch fish from the water like
a giant kite, not plunging like an osprey.
Spends much time perched, often very upright, on a crag
or bare tree. Also walks on ground near water, or on ice, stealing food
from other birds of prey, crows, and ravens.

Perched ▼
Leans forward when alert or to feed; big head and bill; bare lower leg

▼ Flight
Long, broad, flat "barn door" wings, protruding head, short tail

ADULT

JUVENILE

ADULT

JUVENILE

JUVENILE

▼ Juvenile male from below
Male markedly smaller, slimmer than female; juvenile streaked below, tail dark with whitish streaks

▲ ▼ Juveniles
Saw-toothed trailing edge, unlike adult

▲ Juvenile female
Female bigger, broader-winged than male at all ages

Marsh Harrier
Circus aeruginosus

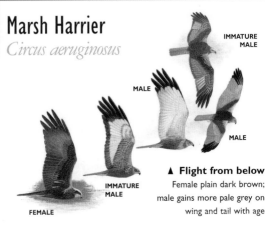

▲ Flight from below
Female plain dark brown;
male gains more pale grey on
wing and tail with age

IMMATURE MALE

MALE

MALE

IMMATURE MALE

FEMALE

48–55cm 19–22in

DISTRIBUTION
Widespread, but
very local; common
only in extensive
marshes, often
near coasts, fewer
in small reedbeds

IDENTIFICATION All harriers characterized by low flight over open spaces, with several slow flaps and long, wavering glides on raised wings. Reedbed habitat a good clue to marsh harrier, but other harriers visit reeds, too; marsh is biggest and broadest-winged, especially bulky female (male more lightly built). Mature male has pale grey inner wing and tail, contrasted with dark back and black wingtips. Female darker, plainer, almost all dark brown (buzzard more patterned; black kite has notched tail, angled wings, pale diagonal band across upperwing, paler patch behind wing angle).

HABITAT Breeds in reedbeds, usually large ones, near pools, and shallow lagoons. Also feeds over adjacent farmland and open damp grassland. Occupies similar habitats in winter.

BEHAVIOUR In spring marsh harriers display high over reedbeds; males pass food to females in flight when they are nesting. Otherwise usually seen flying low, beating steadily into the wind, searching for prey such as a small songbird, a coot, or a duckling which it can surprise and catch with a short, fast chase or dive. Also tends to perch inconspicuously on tops of bushes, on fence posts, or on other vantage points with a view over the marsh.

Flight profiles ▼
Soars with wings well spread and pushed forward, like buzzard; tail rounded unlike black kite; flies with wings raised in distinct V

From below ▼
Two-tone underwing on juvenile male (left), but no white patch behind bend of wing

◄ Juvenile
Pale crown and throat; wing dark, but paler feather edges give more or less scaly look

▲ Female from above
Dark chocolate brown, with pale yellow-buff crown and forewing patch variably prominent

Adult male ▼
Striking black, brown, rufous, buff, and grey when fully mature; both sexes have long, thin, yellow legs

MALE

FEMALE

JUVENILE

Adult female ▲
Dark brown; creamy-buff on wing edge and head, dark band through eye

Hen Harrier
Circus cyaneus

MALE

FEMALE

▲ **Perched**
Male bluish-grey; female dark
brown; long, yellow legs

43–50cm 17–20in

DISTRIBUTION
In summer locally,
thinly spread in N
Europe, mostly on
moors; more widely
in winter on fields,
marshes

IDENTIFICATION Medium-sized harrier, female broader-winged than male. Both broader-winged, with blunter, shorter wingtip, than Montagu's harrier, but females very alike. Male has white rump, and dark trailing edge to plain grey inner wing (male Montagu's has grey rump, black bars below wing and black bar above inner wing, streaked underbody). Female has banded tail, white rump, slight owl-like ruff around lower face (female Montagu's similar but slimmer, with less of a ruff and more distinct, paler crescents above and below eye).

HABITAT Breeds on open moorland, especially with deep heather or rushes; also farmland in some areas, nesting in cereal fields.

◄ **Flight profile**
Glides with wings raised in shallow V

▼ Juvenile female
Rufous-buff below; barred underwing darkest near body; white rump

▼ Adult female
Pale grey-buff, barred on underwing; white rump; banded tail

▼ From above
White rump in all plumages

MALE

JUVENILE

FEMALE

▼ From below
Male slimmer than female; adult white with grey chest, black wingtips, dark hindwing; juvenile more streaked than young Montagu's

ADULT MALE

JUVENILE MALE

In winter on low-lying grassy marshes, saltmarshes near estuaries, and over sand dunes, damp pastures, and other open ground.

BEHAVIOUR All harriers hunt by flying low, but quite fast, with a series of wingbeats between glides on raised wings. The hen harrier chases small birds, or stoops quickly to snatch a bird or rodent in a low-level attack. Perches for long periods on stumps or hummocks, often inconspicuous. In spring the males display with a bouncing, dancing flight over the nesting area. The male hunts for food for the female, and delivers it with a "food pass", the female flying up from the nest to take it in her feet while rolling over beneath the male.

Buzzard
Buteo buteo

IDENTIFICATION A medium-large bird of prey, bigger than a crow and impressive in flight, with long, broad, rounded wings. Variable but typically brown above, cream below with dark streaks and a darker breast band; barred underwing shows a pale area beyond a dark wrist patch. Northern birds often paler, some almost all creamy-buff; others may have a whitish rump or tail base, recalling rough-legged buzzard, but common buzzard has quite stiff, slightly jerky wingbeats (rough-legged's flight more elastic, closer to honey buzzard's action). Loud, ringing "mewing" call.

50–57cm 20–22in

DISTRIBUTION Widespread, but in N Europe mainly a summer visitor; large numbers on coasts of NW Europe in winter, on farmland and marshes

HABITAT All kinds of open or wooded landscapes, from coastal and inland cliffs to lowland forest; often over open coastal areas.

BEHAVIOUR Commonly seen soaring high up, drifting in circles on raised wings, sometimes calling with challenging *peeyaaa*. Also often perched on telegraph pole, fence post, or even on the ground, looking for prey (from beetles and earthworms to birds and rabbits). In spring small flocks gather in favourite fields, or groups of five or six soar together over woodland nesting areas.

▼ **Perched**
Typical (right), with pale U-shape under dark chest; pale types (left) frequent

▼ **Juvenile**
Juvenile has even, narrow bands on tail (left feather); adult has broader band at tip (right feather)

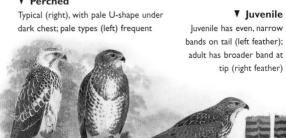

▼ Flight from below

Broad, short head; long, wide wings with dark patch at wrist; rather short, closely barred tail; very variable patterns; tail does not have white base, black band, like rough-legged buzzard

JUVENILE

TYPICAL ADULT FEMALE

PALE JUVENILE FEMALE

GLIDING

▲ Flight from above

Very variable; typically dark and quite uniform brown (right), but may be patched with creamy-buff to white (left)

▼ Flight profiles

Soars with wings in V; glides on flatter, angled wings between jerky wingbeats

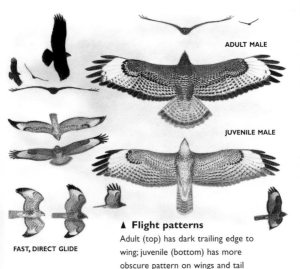

ADULT MALE

JUVENILE MALE

FAST, DIRECT GLIDE

▲ Flight patterns

Adult (top) has dark trailing edge to wing; juvenile (bottom) has more obscure pattern on wings and tail

Rough-legged Buzzard
Buteo lagopus

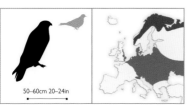

50–60cm 20–24in

DISTRIBUTION
Northern breeding
bird on moors,
tundra; more
widespread, but
usually scarce,
in winter

IDENTIFICATION A big buzzard, but with a rather small, delicate head; feathered legs are usually very hard to see. The female, especially, has a blackish belly patch (pale on adult males) and white tail with a broad black band at the tip (several narrower bands on males and a duller, browner band on juveniles). The upperwing has a whitish "flash" towards the tip; the head is usually pale, "frosted" whitish. Common buzzards may have some of these features and cause confusion, but are stockier, shorter-winged, with a stiffer flight action (rough-legged has a softer, smoother action). Both may hover like clumsy kestrels, the rough-legged more frequently and expertly than most common buzzards.

HABITAT Open ground in tundra and mountain areas; in winter, grassland and marshes near low-lying coasts.

BEHAVIOUR Spends long periods perched on poles or trees. Hunts small mammals by flying low over open ground, or hovering.

◀ Flight
Dark, with paler head, whitish
patch towards wingtip above,
blacker wrist patch and belly,
white tail with dark tip

ADULT FEMALE

JUVENILE FEMALE

JUVENILE MALE

Flight shapes ▲

Male slimmer than longer-
winged female; longer tail
than common buzzard

▼ Perched ►

Typical upright stance, pale head and
upper body, black belly; juvenile has
paler eye than adult; male has
shorter wingtips than female

ADULT FEMALE

JUVENILE MALE

JUVENILE

FEMALE   **MALE**   **JUVENILE**

Osprey
Pandion haliaetus

▼ **Flight shapes**
Long, narrow, angled wings, gull-like at distance; short tail

55–65cm 22–26in

DISTRIBUTION
Widespread in N Europe, local S Europe; almost anywhere on migration on coasts, lakes, reservoirs

IDENTIFICATION A large bird of prey, rather eagle-like, but with wings kinked upwards at joint in flight, giving distinctive profile. Dark above, white below, with prominent whitish head crossed by black band. Underwing has dark wrist patch and more or less black mottling, especially along mid-section. Tail quite short, with pale, translucent bands. Flight relaxed, with easy beats and smooth glides; hovers before diving for fish.

HABITAT Lakes, rivers, adjacent wooded farmland, and forest clearings; feeds in shallow coastal waters, especially on migration in spring and autumn.

BEHAVIOUR Long periods of inactivity, perched in tree or on pole. Feeds over open water with spectacular headlong dives, entering feet-first with big splash and emerging with fish held in long, curved, very sharp claws. Shakes water from feathers and typically carries fish head-first to feeding perch.

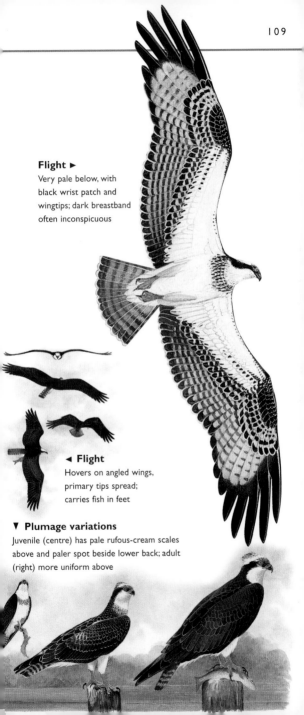

Flight ►
Very pale below, with
black wrist patch and
wingtips; dark breastband
often inconspicuous

◄ Flight
Hovers on angled wings,
primary tips spread;
carries fish in feet

▼ Plumage variations
Juvenile (centre) has pale rufous-cream scales
above and paler spot beside lower back; adult
(right) more uniform above

Kestrel
Falco tinnunculus

MALE

FEMALE

31–37cm 12–15in

▲ Perched
Often upright, rather large-headed,
long-tailed, wingtips fall short of tail
tip; may look more hunched and
broad-shouldered

DISTRIBUTION
Widespread and
common on farmland,
moors, heaths; frequent
migrant on coasts,
especially on rough
ground, headlands,
coastal heaths

IDENTIFICATION Small, long-winged falcon, with long, slender tail, blunt head. Frequently hovers as if suspended on a string, far more than any other bird of prey. Direct flight quite slow, floppy, but can be acrobatic and dashing in wind. Always has contrasting pale inner wing and dark outer wing. Male's grey tail distinctive in flight.

HABITAT Open ground of all kinds, from farmland and moors to coastal marshes; often on rough grassy areas near roads, railways, along cliff tops. Migrants frequently follow coasts.

BEHAVIOUR Frequent hovering is most distinctive characteristic, but often perches, looking for food, on overhead wire or high post or branch, dropping to ground to seize prey.

◄ Flight
Male (left) has grey tail,
female all rufous-brown;
both show dark outer
wing, pale inner wing

Flight shapes ▶

Variable according to action: sharp-
winged in glide and direct, fast flight
with wings angled back; broad, blunt
wingtip when soaring; typically narrow
tail except when soaring and hovering

MALE

FEMALE

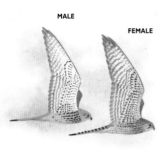

Flight from below ▲

Looks darker-bodied, paler-winged
unless in dull light, when may look
dark and dull overall; note greyer
wingtip, dark tailband

▼ Female

Rusty-brown, barred black;
underside rich buff; tail
narrowly barred

Male ▶

Blue-grey head, small bill,
slight moustache; back
spotted black; tail grey
with black band

Merlin
Falco columbarius

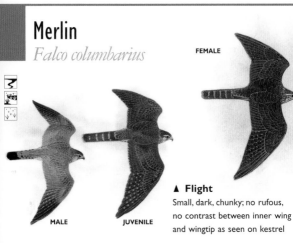

FEMALE

MALE

JUVENILE

▲ **Flight**
Small, dark, chunky; no rufous, no contrast between inner wing and wingtip as seen on kestrel

25–30cm 10–12in

DISTRIBUTION
Scarce and local breeder, wanders widely in winter, especially near coasts, on fields, marshes

IDENTIFICATION Smallest European falcon, male size of mistle thrush, female close to kestrel, but stockier, broader-shouldered, and shorter-tailed. Shape, with broad-based wings, similar to fast-flying sparrowhawk, but longer wings and shorter tail usually evident. Male's colours also recall male sparrowhawk, but has black tailband, streaked underside, dark eye, and longer wingtip. Female earth-brown, more uniform above; less rufous than kestrel, lacks dark moustache of peregrine. Fast, low flight with rapid, deep wingbeats or sharp flicks of swept-back wings in pursuit of small birds.

HABITAT Breeds on moors in the uplands in summer. In winter occurs on all kinds of open ground, including farmland, heaths, coastal marshes, dunes, and in the general vicinity of estuaries, wherever small birds are abundant.

BEHAVIOUR A dashing little falcon when chasing its prey, but otherwise spends much time sitting motionless on a low perch, such as a fence post, a clump of earth, or a rock. It is most often seen flying by, keeping close to the ground, and it does not generally soar up higher as do most other birds of prey.

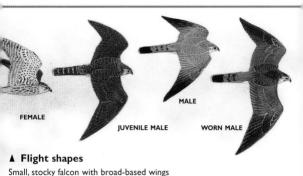

FEMALE

MALE

JUVENILE MALE

WORN MALE

▲ Flight shapes

Small, stocky falcon with broad-based wings tapering to sharp, whippy, swept-back point; medium-length tail, narrow when closed

Juvenile female tail ▶

Tail closely barred brown and cream; adult female similar, but with fewer, broader cream bars

▼ Adult male

Bluish above, bright buff to orange-buff below, streaked

JUVENILE FEMALE

▼ Dashing flight

Chases prey in long, fast, acrobatic pursuit, usually low over ground

▲ Adult female

Earth-brown, streaked and barred below, tail banded cream and brown; weak head pattern

Eleonora's Falcon
Falco eleonorae

36–42cm 14–17in

DISTRIBUTION
Extremely local,
on Mediterranean
coasts and islands,
late spring to late
autumn

IDENTIFICATION Similar to peregrine and hobby. More slender than peregrine, especially across rump and base of tail; pale form much darker on belly. Bigger than hobby, with longer and broader wings; darker beneath, but pale form not easy to separate. Dark form easier, as only European falcon that looks entirely sooty-grey overall (apart from very rare melanistic kestrel and smaller, red-thighed, red-footed falcon). Long wings taper to scythe-like tips; tail slightly wedge-shaped when fanned.

HABITAT Cliffs and offshore stacks, adjacent mountainous areas. Also low-lying coastal marshes and lagoons.

BEHAVIOUR Breeds late in summer to feed young on small autumn migrants such as warblers, swallows, martins; also catches insects and birds over marshes. Social, breeding and hunting in small groups (hobby can also feed in groups). Dashing, acrobatic flight, often soaring out over the sea.

Two forms ▼
Pale form has white throat and neck,
black moustache; dark form all dark
grey-brown

JUVENILE

PALE FORM

DARK FORM

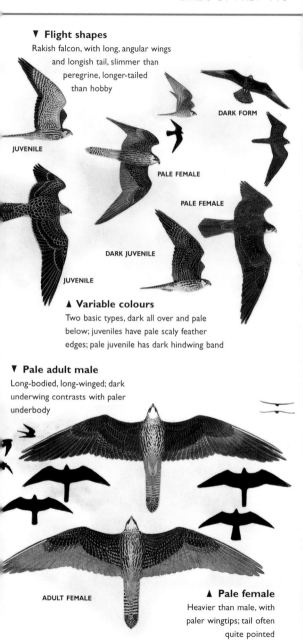

▼ Flight shapes
Rakish falcon, with long, angular wings and longish tail, slimmer than peregrine, longer-tailed than hobby

JUVENILE

DARK FORM

PALE FEMALE

PALE FEMALE

DARK JUVENILE

JUVENILE

▲ Variable colours
Two basic types, dark all over and pale below; juveniles have pale scaly feather edges; pale juvenile has dark hindwing band

▼ Pale adult male
Long-bodied, long-winged; dark underwing contrasts with paler underbody

ADULT FEMALE

▲ Pale female
Heavier than male, with paler wingtips; tail often quite pointed

Peregrine Falcon
Falco peregrinus

JUVENILE

ADULT

JUVENILE

JUVENILE

JUVENILE

▲ **Perched**
Adult bluish-grey above, juvenile brown;
adult barred below, juvenile streaked;
white throat and neck, black moustache

39–50cm 15–20in

DISTRIBUTION
Widespread but
local breeder;
great wanderer
in winter, especially
around coasts, on
marshes, and cliffs

IDENTIFICATION A big falcon with a strong, muscular body, wide-based wings tapered to point, and short, wide tail. Typically anchor-like silhouette. Female bigger and heavier than male, which can recall slighter hobby at times. Bold white patch on throat/neck against broad, lobe-shaped black moustache evident at long range. Crosswise bars beneath visible only at close range; tends to look white on breast, grey below, often with tinge of pink-buff. From above, broad rump often paler than back and tail. Juvenile shares basic shape and head pattern, but is streaked underneath with broad splashes of black. Flies with deep, fast, regular wingbeats, especially in fast chase, or glides and soars on flat wings. Dives on prey at great speed (hobby can be similar), or dives past, then swoops up again to take it from below.

▼ Flight impressions

Big, broad-winged, with wide shoulders and particularly broad rump/tail base; wings quite blunt at full stretch, but tapered to sharp point when angled back, or held in smooth arc to give distinctive anchor shape

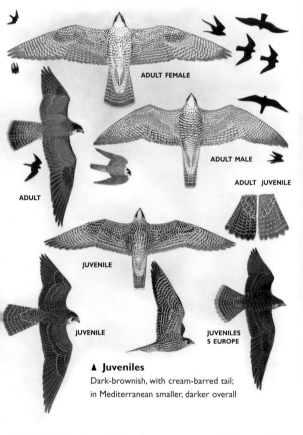

ADULT FEMALE

ADULT MALE

ADULT JUVENILE

ADULT

JUVENILE

JUVENILE

JUVENILE

JUVENILES
S EUROPE

▲ Juveniles

Dark-brownish, with cream-barred tail; in Mediterranean smaller, darker overall

HABITAT Breeds on cliffs, rocks, sometimes city buildings, tall chimneys, or towers. Widespread in winter on low-lying coasts, often around estuaries, where wildfowl and waders provide prey.

BEHAVIOUR Perches motionless for hours on cliff ledge, building, post, or even on the ground. Circles high up on lookout for prey, then moves towards it in high, fast, accelerating flight before chase or "stoop": a very fast dive with closed wings. Often takes pigeons around cities, near coastal cliffs, or even over the sea.

Coot
Fulica atra

◄ Facial shield
Broad, white facial shield and white bill unique, except for very rare crested coot in Spain

FEMALE

MALE

36–38cm 14–15in

DISTRIBUTION
Widespread breeding bird on inland waters; in winter on sheltered coasts and adjacent grassy areas, floods

IDENTIFICATION Round-backed, short-tailed, round-headed water bird, also often seen on nearby land, usually in small flocks. Dark plumage and white bill distinctive (crested coot, very rare in Mediterranean area, similar but has small red knobs on top of wedge-shaped, less rounded, white shield). In flight, or when scurrying across water with open wings, pale trailing edge to wing characteristic. Loud, abrupt metallic or ringing calls.

HABITAT Variety of freshwater lakes, rivers, pools, and marshes; occasionally on the sea. Frequently occurs on grassy areas near bays and marinas.

BEHAVIOUR Coots are always social birds, breeding in loose groups and making big nests at the water's edge. At all other times they form small to large flocks, often with hundreds and sometimes thousands gathering on larger reservoirs or on open grassland close to water. If disturbed, they run or fly to the safety of water, but if alarmed by shooting, or powerboats, flocks can sometimes fly up and circle around, flying higher than usual, soon tiring. They feed by grazing or by diving under from the water surface to find aquatic plants, occasionally small fish, tadpoles, and insects. They bring large quantities of weed to the surface.

▲ Clumsy flight
Outstretched head, long, trailing feet, round wings; typically flies low, but flocks may circle high when disturbed

◄ Alarmed
Runs across ground with half-open wings to nearest water

▼ On water
Forms flocks almost all year round, often near sheltered edges of pools

▼ Adult and young
Young birds follow parents, calling to be fed with loud whistles

▼ Adults
Slaty-grey, blacker on head and neck; white bill and shield easy to see at long range; big feet with broadly lobed toes

▼ Immature
White face and underparts of juvenile soon lost, but keeps pale throat or chin for first year

IMMATURE

Oystercatcher
Haematopus ostralegus

40–45cm 16–18in

DISTRIBUTION
Chiefly coastal breeder, but also inland in upland river valleys; widespread on coasts in winter

IDENTIFICATION Generally unmistakable; bold black-and-white pattern (in flight, only black-tailed godwit has similar pattern, but not nearly so striking, with browner upperparts; also has long, dark legs extending well beyond tail). Flocks look black with white splashes and dashes of bright orange bills. Drabber in juvenile plumages and also in summer before moult, when even adult may look browner-backed as feathers wear and fade. Loud, abrupt calls, including *kip, kleep,* and *pic-pic-pic,* and *kleep-kleep-kleep-a-kleep* in piercing piping display.

HABITAT Breeds mostly on low-lying rocky coasts and islands, with grassy swards and small sandy beaches; also inland on pastures, riversides, places beside lakes, or flooded gravel pits. All year on coasts of mud, sand, or rock, with abundant shellfish.

BEHAVIOUR An intensely social bird for most of the year, with flocks of hundreds or thousands spreading widely over beaches at low tide, and forming dense gatherings at high tide in traditional safe roosting sites. In summer, pairs set up territories, but still meet and display together in small groups. Often quite tame on beaches, especially when encountered individually or in small groups, but larger flocks tend to be wild and wary, and roosts are easily disturbed.

▼ Social groups
Usually in flocks; small parties call loudly with heads bowed, bills open, and ear-splitting calls

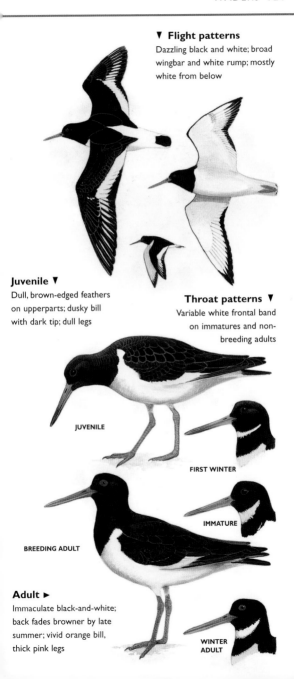

▼ Flight patterns
Dazzling black and white; broad wingbar and white rump; mostly white from below

Juvenile ▼
Dull, brown-edged feathers on upperparts; dusky bill with dark tip; dull legs

Throat patterns ▼
Variable white frontal band on immatures and non-breeding adults

JUVENILE

FIRST WINTER

IMMATURE

BREEDING ADULT

Adult ▶
Immaculate black-and-white; back fades browner by late summer; vivid orange bill, thick pink legs

WINTER ADULT

Black-winged Stilt
Himantopus himantopus

33–38cm 13–15in

DISTRIBUTION
Local and widely
scattered, spring to
autumn, rare at other
times; core range is
around Mediterranean

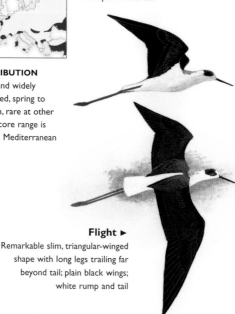

Juvenile ▲
Dull brownish-grey tinge above, with pale
trailing edge to wing; long white V on back
from pure white tail

Flight ▶
Remarkable slim, triangular-winged
shape with long legs trailing far
beyond tail; plain black wings;
white rump and tail

◄ Head patterns
Variable within age groups
and sexes; typically darker
in summer (top) and
whiter in winter (bottom);
males typically have more
black, but much overlap

IDENTIFICATION Unmistakable if seen well, but may swim or wade in deep water, hiding legs from view. Needle-fine black bill, small head, long wingtips extending beyond tail, and black-and-white appearance distinctive. In flight long legs trailed, feet often crossed over; dark underwing with white triangle at base noticeable. Loud chattering and scolding calls, tern-like in quality.

HABITAT Classic habitat is Mediterranean shore saltpans and lagoons. Also various shallow lakes, marshes with small pools, flooded pits, also sometimes open sandy shores.

BEHAVIOUR Noisy, nervy birds, easily disturbed, especially in summer if there are young chicks about. Stilts often fly over or even dive at human intruders, and chase other birds, such as crows or birds of prey, with loud calls. They wade deeply, but pick food from the surface of water with their fine bills, or swim like giant phalaropes. Equally often they may be seen on wet mud or in shallow water, when their remarkably long legs are striking. Usually stilts are seen in pairs or family parties, not in larger flocks.

▼ **Adult**
Black-glossed green, browner on female; extremely long, pink legs

ADULT

JUVENILE

▲ **Juvenile**
Dull, greyish head and neck,
pale brown feather fringes
above reduce contrast

ADULT

Avocet
Recurvirostra avosetta

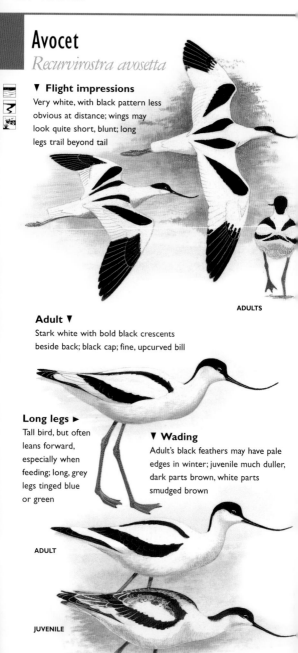

▼ Flight impressions
Very white, with black pattern less
obvious at distance; wings may
look quite short, blunt; long
legs trail beyond tail

ADULTS

Adult ▼
Stark white with bold black crescents
beside back; black cap; fine, upcurved bill

Long legs ►
Tall bird, but often
leans forward,
especially when
feeding; long, grey
legs tinged blue
or green

▼ Wading
Adult's black feathers may have pale
edges in winter; juvenile much duller,
dark parts brown, white parts
smudged brown

ADULT

JUVENILE

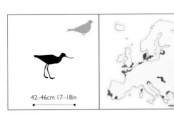

DISTRIBUTION
Most widespread in summer; most birds move to sheltered estuaries farther south and west in winter

42–46cm 17–18in

IDENTIFICATION Easy to tell when seen well: no other similar bird in Europe, with upturned bill, black cap, and crescents on back, on otherwise clean white plumage. At long range, however, gleaming white appearance may make it easy to overlook among gulls feeding on an estuary. Juvenile duller, sullied by brown feather edgings, but basic pattern always evident and bill shape obvious.

HABITAT Breeds on shallow lagoons with shingly or muddy islands, with plentiful invertebrate food such as tiny shrimps; increasingly breeds on muddy pools inland. In winter, feeds on muddy estuaries with wide channels and shallow creeks.

BEHAVIOUR Avocets are mostly found in flocks, even in the breeding season when they nest in small colonies, although isolated pairs may colonize new sites before consolidation by larger groups. They feed by walking slowly forward in shallow water or on wet, glistening mud, sweeping their bills sideways through the surface ooze to extract minute aquatic organisms. In winter they may feed in quite dense flocks of tens or even hundreds in favoured places, such as at the edge of a channel in the middle of an estuary as the tide recedes. In such situations avocets are active and lively birds, dashing into the water and constantly moving position.

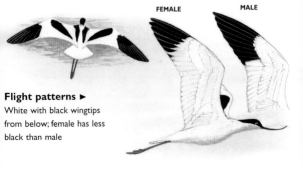

FEMALE MALE

Flight patterns ▶
White with black wingtips from below; female has less black than male

Ringed Plover
Charadrius hiaticula

◄ Variations
Adults (left and right) boldly marked; juvenile (centre) much less so, duller

DISTRIBUTION
Most breed on the coast, but also increasingly inland; in winter mostly on coasts, especially estuaries

18–20cm 7–8in

Summer adult male ▼
Handsome, immaculate brown above, white below, with black headbands and breastbands; orange legs and base of bill

▼ Winter
Breastband slightly narrower, browner, less clear-cut; paler feather edges

FANNED TAIL

▲ Adult female
Black areas duller than male, less extensive; tail shorter (compare tail/wingtips with male above)

▲ Juvenile
Brown cap, white above eye, brown mask and breastband; legs duller, yellower than adult, bill black

▼ **Flight from above**
Long white wing stripe; dark rump
and tail with white sides, blacker
"blob" on tip of tail; longer tail
and broader wings than dunlin

ADULT

JUVENILE

IDENTIFICATION A neat, small plover. Plovers are short-billed, rounded, short-legged waders compared with the longer-billed sandpipers such as the dunlin and stints. The ringed plover's orange-based bill and orange legs are distinctive; the black "ring" on the chest is shared only by the little ringed plover (more restricted to freshwater, with a black bill, dull legs, and plainer upperwing). Rich, fluty *too-li* or *too-ip* call.

From below ▼
Juvenile is pale,
with incomplete
breastband; adult
has full black band

JUVENILE

ADULT

HABITAT All kinds of watersides, from flooded pits, muddy reservoir edges, and lagoons to shingle, sandy, and muddy shores. In winter occurs mostly on larger estuaries.

BEHAVIOUR A typical plover in its movements, with a "stop-start" action as it moves across a beach: running, then pausing to look around, or tilt forward to pick up food. Often solitary, but more usually in small groups, gathering into flocks of scores or hundreds at high-tide roosts, often in close proximity to other waders, including dunlins and sanderlings.

Kentish Plover
Charadrius alexandrinus

▼ **Flight pattern**
White wing bar, white sides
to brown tail

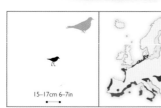

15–17cm 6–7in

DISTRIBUTION
Mostly scarce and
very local, most
widespread in
Mediterranean area;
rare migrant north
of main range

IDENTIFICATION A small, pale plover, usually easy to identify, but can be confused with juvenile ringed and little ringed plovers. Little ringed has no white wing bar and pale legs (although its bill is mostly black). Juvenile ringed has a clearly defined dark cap, a thicker bill, and broader dark patches at the sides of the breast, as well as pale legs. Kentish is best identified by black legs if the head and breast pattern leave any doubt. Male in summer is obvious with rufous cap and black patches. Calls include a sharp *whit* or ticking note, and a short, clear whistle.

HABITAT Mostly found on sandy beaches, as well as sandy shores, tracks, and embankments around salt pans, lagoons, and even building sites.

BEHAVIOUR Like other plovers, the Kentish plover has a run-stop-tilt-run action as it trips along a sandy beach. It is fairly tame, but always alert and rather nervous, especially in summer when its nesting areas are often subject to frequent disturbance. It is often found among groups of other waders, especially ringed plovers at high-tide roosts, but not generally in flocks of more than four or five at a time of its own species.

▲ **Variant**
Rarely, may show
yellowish legs;
typically legs are
black or dark grey

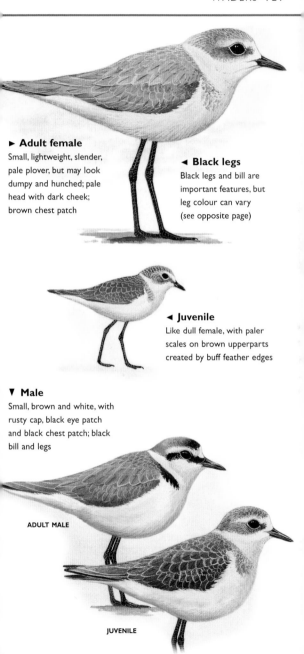

▶ Adult female
Small, lightweight, slender, pale plover, but may look dumpy and hunched; pale head with dark cheek; brown chest patch

◀ Black legs
Black legs and bill are important features, but leg colour can vary (see opposite page)

◀ Juvenile
Like dull female, with paler scales on brown upperparts created by buff feather edges

▼ Male
Small, brown and white, with rusty cap, black eye patch and black chest patch; black bill and legs

ADULT MALE

JUVENILE

Golden Plover
Pluvialis apricaria

26–29cm 10–11 in

DISTRIBUTION
Widespread but local breeder in north; more southerly in winter, often on traditional pastures

◄ Winter flocks
Typical walk-stop-tilt feeding action; spread out over flat fields

IDENTIFICATION A medium-sized, rounded, small-headed plover with short bill and long legs. Spangled black and yellow above, looks warm brown in winter with pale underside, in summer has black on belly and face. Dark rump, thin wingbar, white underwing. Plaintive *peeeuw* call in flight.

▲ Flight
Round head; dark rump, weak wingbar; white underwing and belly often striking

HABITAT Breeds on high moors with short or burnt heather, or short grass. On saltmarshes, ploughed fields, pastures in winter.

▼ Two races
Northern race (centre) blacker on face than southern (right) in summer; identical in winter (left)

BEHAVIOUR Forms big winter flocks, often hundreds or thousands strong, roosting in dense groups, but spreading out evenly over low ground to feed; flies in long lines and V-shapes. Often with lapwings, but they separate in the air, lapwings flying less quickly and directly. Uses typical plover forward tilt to pick food from the ground; often chased by gulls eager to steal worms. In summer typically in pairs, or a few pairs breeding in loose groups.

▼ Adults
Smart black-, white-and-grey in summer, moulting (inset) to dull grey in winter; stout black bill, large dark eye, black legs

Grey Plover
Pluvialis squatarola

WINTER

SUMMER

▼ Flight
White rump, wing bar, unique black "wing pit" patch

WINTER

SUMMER

▲ Juvenile
Spangled grey, washed buff, resembling golden, but less brownish, bill and head bigger, different flight pattern

27–30cm 11–12in

DISTRIBUTION
Arctic tundra breeder, widespread on coasts, but rare inland from late summer to late spring

IDENTIFICATION Quite large plover, bigger than golden, with stouter body and bigger bill, but similar plumage patterns. Black "wing pit" diagnostic in flight, combined with white wingbar and rump (dark rump on golden). At distance can be confused with other waders, but looks dark, hunched, and short-billed; at close range, exquisite patterns visible. Distinctive triple *tee-u-wee* whistle.

HABITAT Mostly found on muddy estuaries and beaches.

BEHAVIOUR Feeds in loose groups, scattered over mud, but gathers in large flocks with other waders at high tide.

Lapwing
Vanellus vanellus

▼ Flight
Broad, wide-tipped wings, dark upperparts in sharp contrast with white underside

▲ Flight patterns
Male (left) has wider outer wing than female (above); dark green looks blackish at distance or in poor light, white rump obvious

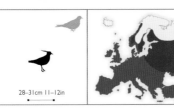

28–31cm 11–12in

DISTRIBUTION
Widespread, but local and declining; in winter large flocks roam widely over lowland areas, coastal marshes

IDENTIFICATION Unique in Europe, a wading bird (although often on dry land) with a thin crest and broad, rounded wings. Short bill and medium-length legs typical of plovers, as is tilting feeding action. Black breastband against white belly makes identification easy in dull light of winter, when upperside looks dull and dark. Various nasal *peet* and *peewit* calls.

HABITAT Breeds on lower moors, rough damp commons, arable land, and short-cropped coastal marshes. In autumn often beside lakes and reservoirs. In winter on fields, saltmarshes, and other low, damp, open ground, sometimes in suburban fields, even on flat roofs.

BEHAVIOUR Breeds in small groups of a few pairs, displaying with wild, thrashing flight and nasal, ecstatic song. At other times usually in flocks, from a few scores to thousands strong. Disperses over flat ground when feeding, but gathers into tight flocks to rest and sleep. Flies in erratic packs with slow, flickering action.

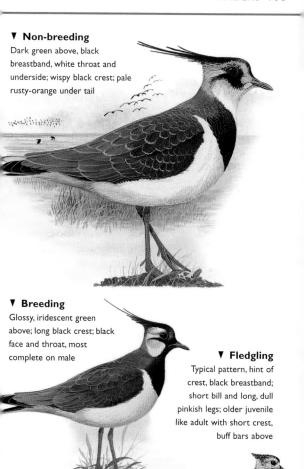

▼ Non-breeding
Dark green above, black breastband, white throat and underside; wispy black crest; pale rusty-orange under tail

▼ Breeding
Glossy, iridescent green above; long black crest; black face and throat, most complete on male

▼ Fledgling
Typical pattern, hint of crest, black breastband; short bill and long, dull pinkish legs; older juvenile like adult with short crest, buff bars above

Winter group ▼
Female (left) has narrower breastband than male (centre); white throat conspicuous; stark white underside striking at rest and in flight

Knot
Calidris canutus

23–27cm 9–11in

DISTRIBUTION
Arctic breeder;
from around July
to May widespread
on coasts, especially
larger estuaries,
rare inland

▼ Plumage patterns
Winter (left and below) grey with paler
rump, fine whitish wingbar; breeding
plumage (right) orange below

Flight ▲
Shortish bill, stocky body; looks
sturdy, middle-sized, larger than dunlin,
but smaller than redshank; square,
shortish tail, feet do not show behind

▼ Autumn adults
Change from breeding orange
to winter grey, with various
patchy stages in between

▼ Breeding adult
Becomes deep orange or
rufous in spring, with black- and
chestnut-spangled back; much
smaller, shorter-legged, than
similarly coloured godwits

IDENTIFICATION In winter the best clue is its relative lack of features, combined with medium-small size and rather short legs and bill. Looks dull, rather pale grey (grey plover often looks darker, round-shouldered, thick-billed; redshank is larger, browner, longer-legged). Dull pale grey rump distinctive in flight. Spring adult quite different in clean, bright orange, rump speckled or barred, but note bill and leg details. Usually silent or makes low, short notes.

HABITAT Most knots are found on large, open beaches of mud and sand, but small numbers are scattered on narrower beaches and even flat, weedy rocks; occasionally appears beside lakes inland.

BEHAVIOUR One of the most social of waders, forming dense flocks where it is most common, even feeding in large groups that advance slowly across the beach like a grey tide. In flight, these flocks of hundreds or thousands perform spectacular coordinated manoeuvres, looking like waving columns of smoke at a distance (beware dunlins which can look similar, but move more quickly, at times – but rarely – in the same huge numbers as the biggest flocks of knots, which can number tens of thousands).

▼ **Winter**
Nondescript pale grey, with whiter line over eye, paler underside; medium-short bill, medium-short pale legs

▼ **Juvenile (lower)**
Young bird in autumn has scaly pattern above, fine streaks below, washed peachy-buff

SUMMER

WINTER

JUVENILE

WINTER

WINTER

Sanderling
Calidris alba

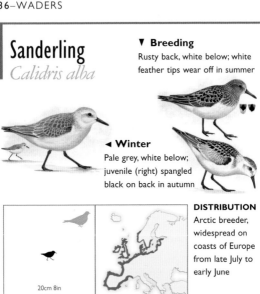

▼ Breeding
Rusty back, white below; white
feather tips wear off in summer

◄ Winter
Pale grey, white below;
juvenile (right) spangled
black on back in autumn

20cm 8in

DISTRIBUTION
Arctic breeder,
widespread on
coasts of Europe
from late July to
early June

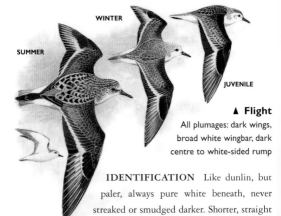

WINTER

SUMMER

JUVENILE

▲ Flight
All plumages: dark wings,
broad white wingbar, dark
centre to white-sided rump

IDENTIFICATION Like dunlin, but
paler, always pure white beneath, never
streaked or smudged darker. Shorter, straight
bill, blacker legs, darker wings with broader
white stripe. Bigger than little stint, without pale V on back. Runs
quickly over flat beaches, often at water's edge. Calls hard *plit* or *kit*.

HABITAT Typically on flat sandy or silty beaches, less often on
open mudflats, sometimes on flat rocks; occasional by reservoirs
inland, especially in May, less so in autumn.

BEHAVIOUR An active shoreline wader, typically running in and
out with advancing and receding waves, but will also feed more
sedately on open mud or sand; roosts in tight-packed groups.

Little Stint
Calidris minuta

WINTER

AUTUMN

◄ **Juvenile**
Common in autumn; rusty above with pale V on back, white below, buff on sides of breast; thin white wingbar at all seasons, dark-centred rump, grey tail

DISTRIBUTION
Arctic breeder; S E Europe in spring, more westerly in autumn, often inland; rare in winter

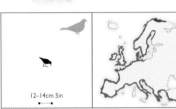

12–14cm 5in

RUMP/TAIL

▲ **Spring adult**
Chequered red/black above, faint pale V; always pure white beneath; black legs; short black bill

IDENTIFICATION Tiny, active wader, smaller than dunlin, barely wagtail-sized. Always white beneath; autumn juvenile bright, well patterned above with red-brown, cream, and black, and distinct buff-white V on back. Winter adult plain grey. Short black legs and bill helpful. Call short, sharp *tit* or *tit-it*.

HABITAT Mostly shallow lagoons, pools on marshes, edges of reservoirs inland, especially with soft mud, but also on mudflats and coastal creeks.

BEHAVIOUR A bird of shallow water and firm muddy or sandy shores, not wading so frequently as dunlin or curlew sandpiper, nor so quick-footed as sanderling. Picks food from surface with quick action, short runs, and occasional pauses. Quick to fly off if disturbed, but often not going far.

▲ **Seasonal changes**
Juvenile (top), summer adult (middle), winter (bottom)

Curlew Sandpiper
Calidris ferruginea

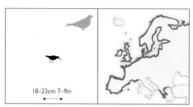

18–23cm 7–9in

DISTRIBUTION
Arctic breeder; migrates north in April/May, returns more westerly in July/August, juveniles later

IDENTIFICATION Small but elegant wader, a little larger than dunlin (often seen together), much bigger than little stint. Long, fine, smoothly curved bill, and longer legs than dunlin. Spring adults have frosty white feather edges which wear off to reveal dark red below. Autumn adults paler, greyer, with remnant patches of red. Juveniles in autumn very smart: scaly above, bright buff on chest. All have wide white band above tail. Call soft, pleasing *chirrup*.

HABITAT Shallow lagoons, creeks, edges of inland waters.

BEHAVIOUR Much like dunlin, but wades more deeply at times; juveniles often very tame. Sociable where common.

▼ **Autumn**
Adult often blotchy between summer and winter; juveniles clean, bright, peachy-buff on breast

▼ **Flight**
Typical small wader wingbar, but distinctive broad white band above tail (less clear in summer)

JUVENILE

WINTER

SUMMER

WINTER

Purple Sandpiper
Calidris maritima

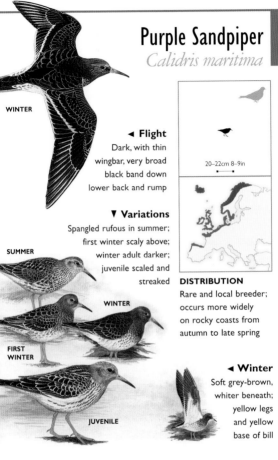

WINTER

◄ **Flight**
Dark, with thin wingbar, very broad black band down lower back and rump

20–22cm 8–9in

▼ **Variations**
Spangled rufous in summer; first winter scaly above; winter adult darker; juvenile scaled and streaked

SUMMER

WINTER

FIRST WINTER

JUVENILE

DISTRIBUTION
Rare and local breeder; occurs more widely on rocky coasts from autumn to late spring

◄ **Winter**
Soft grey-brown, whiter beneath; yellow legs and yellow base of bill

IDENTIFICATION Slightly larger than dunlin; a dark, rather grey wader, in winter with paler scaly edges to feathers of upperparts, whiter chin and eye-ring on plain face, dark breast blending into streaked flanks. Fine-tipped bill has touch of yellow at base, legs pale dull yellow to orange-yellow. Distinctive broad black band down rump in flight. Call sharp *kit* or *weet*.

HABITAT Mostly low, rocky shores, often with turnstones; sometimes on wide, flat rock shelves, usually on weedy rocks washed by waves and in weedy gullies. Also around concrete or metal piles, piers, and breakwaters, even on otherwise sandy or muddy beaches.

BEHAVIOUR Rather quiet, but often moved about by rising tide or breaking waves; usually tame, unless with more nervous species.

Dunlin
Calidris alpina

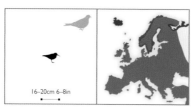

16–20cm 6–8in

DISTRIBUTION
Local breeder on high moors, low marshes, and coastal areas; widespread from July to May, especially on coasts

IDENTIFICATION Small, round-shouldered, often common wader, a standard against which other small waders can be judged. Has shortish, dark grey legs and a rather fine-tipped, slightly curved bill (legs blacker, bill straighter, on both sanderling and scarcer little stint). Black belly and rufous back in summer are unique. In autumn, juvenile is a bright bird, with a pale V on its back, smudgy streaks on sides. Winter birds nondescript, white below, best identified by bill shape, thin, reedy *trreee* call, and the fact that dunlins are usually most common small waders on estuaries and beside lakes.

▼ Flight
Small, neat, fast; sharp wings, pointed bill

WINTER

JUVENILE

SUMMER

EARLY WINTER JUVENILE

HABITAT Breeds on moors; otherwise on all kinds of coasts and beside inland waters, especially on muddy estuaries and beaches.

BEHAVIOUR Slightly sluggish small wader, often in large flocks, especially at high tide when it can be found roosting in packs mixed with sanderlings, knots, and ringed plovers. At low tide disperses widely over beaches, feeding singly or in small, loose groups. Also found inland and on shallow pools anywhere near the coast, especially in spring and autumn, but also all winter if there is a muddy shoreline and shallow water.

◄ Flight patterns
Quick, compact, sharp-winged; thin white wing stripe; white sides to dark-centred rump

▼ Summer
Rusty back; squared black belly patch; grey breast

ADULT WINTER

JUVENILE

▼ Autumn
Adults and juveniles moult into duller grey-brown on back; juveniles bright, with pale V on back, smudgy streaks on flanks

AUTUMN ADULT

AUTUMN JUVENILE

LITTLE STINT

WINTER ADULT

◄ Winter
Dull brownish-grey, dull chest, white beneath; curved bill

Ruff

Philomachus pugnax

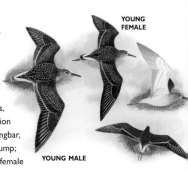

YOUNG FEMALE

YOUNG MALE

► **Flight**
Broad-based, long wings,
short bill, slight projection
of feet past tail; thin wingbar,
white sides (or V) on rump;
male much larger than female

20–32cm 8–13in

DISTRIBUTION
Very local breeder
on low, wet
pastures, floods;
widespread on
migration, scarce in
winter on coasts

IDENTIFICATION Spring males (not often seen away from breeding areas) varied with exotic ruffs (black, white, rufous, or barred) and crests. Often seen in summer with remnant ruff and reduced crest; in winter some have largely white head and foreparts, and red legs. Smaller females dull, boldly marked in summer, plain and pale-legged in winter (godwits have darker legs, longer bills; knots squatter, with pale rumps; redshanks bright-legged, and with bold white band on wing). Autumn juveniles common on migration: look sandy-ochre or buff on foreparts, with beautifully marked back, dark feathers edged buff or white. Legs usually ochre or greenish in autumn; bill slightly curved. Flight quite relaxed with steady wingbeats, revealing oval white sides to rump. Rarely calls.

HABITAT Breeds on low, damp grassland. In winter on flooded fields and marshes, near estuaries. In spring and autumn beside muddy reservoirs and lakes, on shallow lagoons, rare on open beach.

BEHAVIOUR Typically a freshwater wader, keeping to shallow pools and wet meadows, except in winter when small groups are found near estuaries (most migrate to Africa). Rather sedate, both when feeding (in shallow water or on mud) and in flight, when noticeably less erratic and slower than sandpipers and redshanks. Often in small groups, less often in flocks of tens or scores.

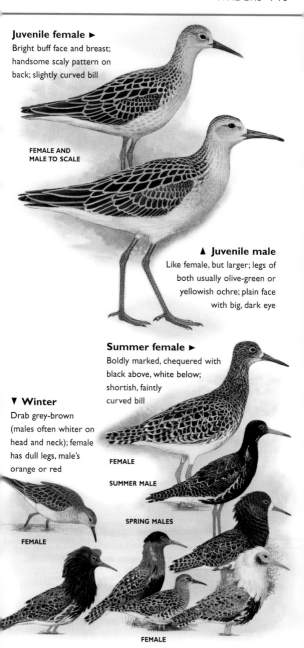

Juvenile female ►
Bright buff face and breast;
handsome scaly pattern on
back; slightly curved bill

**FEMALE AND
MALE TO SCALE**

▲ Juvenile male
Like female, but larger; legs of
both usually olive-green or
yellowish ochre; plain face
with big, dark eye

Summer female ►
Boldly marked, chequered with
black above, white below;
shortish, faintly
curved bill

▼ Winter
Drab grey-brown
(males often whiter on
head and neck); female
has dull legs, male's
orange or red

FEMALE

SUMMER MALE

SPRING MALES

FEMALE

FEMALE

Jack Snipe
Lymnocryptes minimus

17–19cm 7–8in

DISTRIBUTION
Localized breeder;
quite scarce and
highly localized in
winter, wetlands
and upper edges
of saltmarshes

IDENTIFICATION Small snipe, hard to see on ground, typically flies up almost underfoot and escapes in low, circling flight to drop back out of sight. Dark appearance with contrasted back stripes; dark central crown stripe (pale on snipe) may be visible; shorter bill usually obvious. Rarely calls when flushed (snipe usually does so).

HABITAT Waterlogged grass, rushes, muddy places with dense cover, edges of reedbeds with muddy openings; also edge of saltmarsh with wet, muddy spots in dense vegetation.

BEHAVIOUR From autumn to spring keeps to dense cover, usually in scattered groups, but tends to fly up alone or in twos, often close to snipe. Has springy, "bouncy" action on the ground.

▼ **Flight from above**
Small, squat, weak flier; bill shorter than snipe's;
bright back stripes, weak pale trailing edge

Flight from below ▲
Dark underwing contrasts
with white belly

Feeding ►
Small, hunched; dark central head
stripe; broad buff stripes on dark,
green-glossed back; sharp, dark tail

TAIL

▼ Flight
Dashing, long-billed; pale back stripes, strong pale trailing edge to wing; tail round, pale, with orange band

JUVENILE

▲ Underwing
Adult has broad pale bands; juvenile barred grey and white

ADULTS

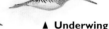

DISTRIBUTION
Local and declining breeder; widespread inland and on coastal marshes in autumn and winter

25–28cm 10–11in

IDENTIFICATION Small wading bird, looks quite chunky, with long, low forehead, strongly striped crown (central stripe pale) and very long, straight, tapered bill. Striped back; bars on flanks contrast with white belly. Short, greenish legs give low, top-heavy appearance on ground. Flies up fast, with rising, often zigzag flight and loud, coarse *scarp* call like tearing cloth.

HABITAT Very wet mud, floods, edges of reeds, shallow pools, and more open mud especially in autumn; also edges of saltmarsh.

BEHAVIOUR Keeps to cover, but much easier to see on ground than jack snipe; flies up high and fast if disturbed.

▼ Juvenile
Less clearly marked, browner than adult

TAIL

◄ Adult
Striped head, barred flanks, white belly; extremely long bill

Black-tailed Godwit
Limosa limosa

36–44cm 14–17in

Flight pattern ▶
Elongated, legs trail
well beyond tail; broad
white wingbar and
band above tail

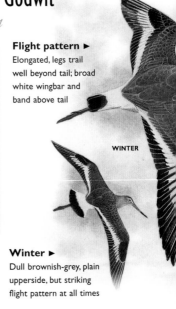

WINTER

DISTRIBUTION
Very localized nester on
wet pastures; in winter
mostly on small, muddy
estuaries, shallow pools
near coast

Winter ▶
Dull brownish-grey, plain
upperside, but striking
flight pattern at all times

IDENTIFICATION   Large, stout, very long-billed wader.
Longer-legged than bar-tailed godwit, with more length above the
joint giving higher stance. Spring and summer adults variably
rufous, females often pale and barred, males richer copper-red, with
barred flanks and white belly (all dark on bar-tailed godwit). Winter
birds greyer, plainer, less streaked than bar-tailed, greyer on chest.
Juvenile in late summer like orange-buff adult, but with scaly
rusty-buff feather edges on back. In flight, easily identified by bold
white bar on wing. Calls nasal *weeka weeka weeka* in spring display;
otherwise a quiet bird.

HABITAT   Breeds on wet, grassy areas, flooded pastures, damp
meadows. In winter in muddy creeks, open mudflats, saltmarshes.

BEHAVIOUR   Migrant flocks rest on wetland areas inland in
spring, then disperse to very localized breeding areas in suitable wet
habitats. Males perform high, diving display flights, rolling over to
show striking pattern. At other times a sedate wader, feeding in
pools, often in flocks. Wades deeply, or stands on open mud leaning
forward with bill almost vertical to feed by probing close to toes.

▼ Breeding plumage
Rufous body, white underwing with narrow, dark trailing edge; grey body in winter

WINTER

SPRING

On ground ▼
Long legs, especially above joint, and very long bill with thick, pinkish base; winter adult plain; first winter more mottled above, buffer on chest

SPRING MALE
ICELAND

WINTER
FEMALE

FIRST WINTER

SPRING MALE

JUVENILE

SPRING FEMALE

Bar-tailed Godwit
Limosa lapponica

33–42cm 13–16in

DISTRIBUTION
Arctic breeder; from July to May widespread on coasts, scarce inland, mostly larger bays and estuaries

▼ **Spring and summer**
Becomes bright, deep copper-orange on head and body, spangled black on back; white underwing; females often paler

▼ **Juvenile**
Late summer juvenile streaked black and buff above, orange-buff on face and neck

SPRING MALE

JUVENILE

WINTER

SPRING MALE

▲ **Winter**
Pale, greyish-brown, slightly streaked above

▲ **Wading**
Very long, slightly upcurved bill; medium length legs

JUVENILE

FIRST WINTER

▲ **Young birds**
Streaked above, long coverts more spotted with buff than on adult, chest more buff

Flight pattern ▼
Wings always plain, with paler edges on flight feathers giving streaky effect; broad, quite short, V-shaped white patch on rump

▼ Juvenile
Juvenile in autumn and first winter bird more streaked than adult, with paler feather edgings above; much more buff on chest

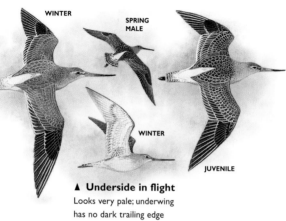

WINTER

SPRING MALE

WINTER

JUVENILE

▲ Underside in flight
Looks very pale; underwing has no dark trailing edge

IDENTIFICATION A medium-large wader, much bigger than grey plover or redshank, but looks small against curlew. At long range in winter looks plain, rather pale, paler-chested than curlew and tending to look more buff on young birds. Very long, finely pointed bill and relatively short legs (best clue compared with black-tailed; stands lower, with long bill giving more forward-leaning, top-heavy effect). In flight, pattern like curlew (very different from black-tailed) with plain wings, white rump. In spring whole underside red (no bars or white belly as on black-tailed). Calls quite loud, nasal *wicka-wicka-wicka*, but mostly quite quiet.

HABITAT Breeds on Arctic tundra. From July to May occurs on many European coasts of all kinds, from flat, open rocks to sand and mud, but mostly on open mudflats. Scarce migrant on inland waters.

BEHAVIOUR Social, often in flocks of hundreds, sometimes thousands, at high-tide roosts. Feeds on mud in widely scattered groups, probing deeply into soft sediment. Flies to roost in long lines and V-shapes, often arriving high up and tumbling down in twisting, acrobatic flight. Roosting groups often close to curlews, grey plovers, and other waders, but tending to keep separate, jostling together as tide rises, reducing the available space.

Whimbrel
Numenius phaeopus

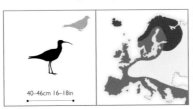

40–46cm 16–18in

DISTRIBUTION
Localized breeder on moors and tundra; widespread migrant in spring and autumn; rare or absent in winter

IDENTIFICATION A large wader, between godwits and curlew in size; a little more compact than curlew, with slightly shorter, more angular bill. Not present in Europe in winter. Looks a little darker than curlew, especially on duller, less tawny-buff chest. Head shows dark stripe each side of narrow pale line on middle of crown (curlew can show similar but much weaker pattern). Darker outer wing and white V on lower back like curlew; flight action quicker. Song rich but less flowing or rippling than curlew; calls are variants of quick, staccato trill, *ti-ti-ti-ti-ti-ti-ti-ti*.

HABITAT Breeds on northern islands, moors, and tundra. Spring and autumn migrants can be found on coasts of all kinds and by areas of water inland, but usually pass through quickly.

BEHAVIOUR Migrant whimbrels, especially in spring, move in flocks; they sometimes gather in scores or even hundreds, but are mostly seen in smaller numbers than curlews and are much more localized. They feed on damp grassland, muddy areas, and on muddy shores, but also on rocky coasts with pools and weed-covered stones.

◀ ▲ Flight
Deep-chested shape, less gull-like than curlew, combined with quicker action

◄ Flight impressions
Stockier, deeper-chested, shorter-tailed, quicker than curlew; looks dark, except for long white V on lower back

▼ On ground
Like smaller curlew; bill shorter, slightly more angled than smoothly curved; strong head stripes; female has longer bill than male

FEMALE

MALE

Adult ▲
Pale notches on feathers (right) wear off in summer to give darker effect overall; female tail shorter

◄ Distant view
Much like curlew; size not obvious unless two are together, or near another large wader for comparison

◄ Resting
Dumpy, hunched shape when relaxed; head stripes not so obvious in side view as head-on

Curlew
Numenius arquata

Flight from below ►
Variably pale underwing, often flashes silvery; underside of body dark in comparison

▲ Distant group
Obvious large size and rangy silhouette, but often hunched, head tucked back, when roosting

50–60cm 20–24in

DISTRIBUTION
Local breeder; widespread migrant and winter bird, especially on floods, marshes, low-lying coasts

IDENTIFICATION The largest wader, a little like a young herring gull with long legs and a long, curved bill; especially gull-like in flight. Streaky brown all over, except for large white V on lower back and rump, and white underwing. Bill long, smoothly downcurved (longest on female); only whimbrel similar, but smaller, with striped head and different call. Curlew tends to look pale at close range, but dark at distance on open beach. Song superb piping, becoming fast, rhythmic, liquid trill. Calls variable, including loud *cur-leee*, drawn-out *whaup*, hard *he-he-hu,* and hoarse, throaty notes.

HABITAT Breeds on wet and dry moors, damp pastures, islands. At other times on grassy fields, muddy estuaries, and beaches of all kinds from flat rock to mud and sand.

BEHAVIOUR A wary wading bird, especially in flocks in winter, which fly off at some distance, although individuals may be much

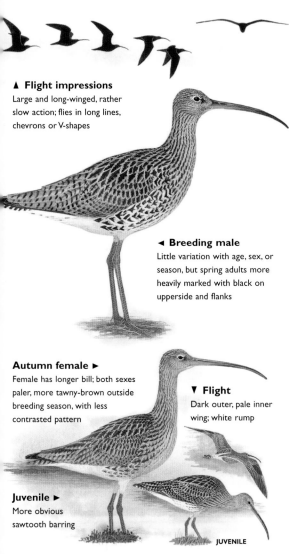

▲ Flight impressions
Large and long-winged, rather slow action; flies in long lines, chevrons or V-shapes

◄ Breeding male
Little variation with age, sex, or season, but spring adults more heavily marked with black on upperside and flanks

Autumn female ►
Female has longer bill; both sexes paler, more tawny-brown outside breeding season, with less contrasted pattern

▼ Flight
Dark outer, pale inner wing; white rump

Juvenile ►
More obvious sawtooth barring

JUVENILE

more approachable. Gathers in large flocks with other waders at high tide; disperses to feed over beaches and fields, walking slowly forward, picking and probing for worms, crabs, and other small creatures. In spring, territorial male flies up, then slowly circles down on raised wings, giving beautiful, trilling song.

Spotted Redshank
Tringa erythropus

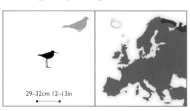

29–32cm 12–13in

DISTRIBUTION
Very local breeder; widespread migrant, inland and on coasts; sparse in winter, on sheltered estuaries

IDENTIFICATION Medium-large, slender wader with long legs and long, fine bill, fractionally downcurved at tip. Bigger than redshank, more slender and thinner-billed than greenshank. In summer uniquely blackish with dark legs. In autumn and winter adult is pale grey and white with bright red leg, red at base of bill, and white stripe above dark line through eye. Autumn juvenile browner, barred on flanks, with similarly striped face pattern, more striking than on redshank. All show dark wings and long, narrow, white oval on back in flight. Legs trail well beyond tail (but sometimes tucked forward). Call is sharp, clearly defined *chew-it*.

HABITAT Breeds in northern forest clearings. On migration feeds in all kinds of fresh water, including coastal pools, and on saltmarsh and estuary creeks. Wintering birds occur on small, often narrow estuaries and muddy channels.

BEHAVIOUR Shy wader, often wading deeply and swimming much more than most similar wading birds. Small feeding flocks can be very active: swimming, up-ending like ducks, and darting after small fish in rapid, erratic runs. Length of bill usually obvious when picking food from water, or probing into water and mud with quick, forward-leaning movement.

◄ Autumn juvenile
Browner than adult, but same head pattern, flight pattern, bill colour, long, red legs, and diagnostic call

▼ Flight patterns
Dark wings, dusky tail, white central oval on back, very white underwing; long legs trail far beyond tail; deep beats of bowed wings

AUTUMN

UNDERSIDE

Breeding plumage ▼
Blackish with white feather edges; these wear off to give striking solid black body in summer (below)

SPRING

▼ Autumn
Black gradually replaced by new pale feathers in progression to winter

▲ Winter
Slaty grey above, speckled with white (pale in bright light), white below; note black and white stripes from bill to eye; long bill, red at base

Redshank
Tringa totanus

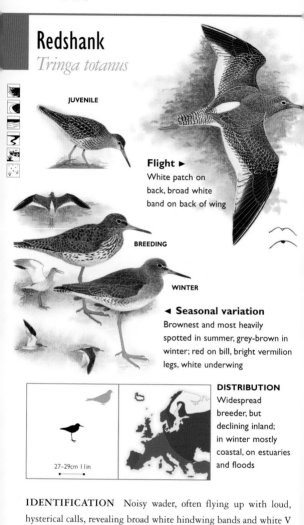

JUVENILE

Flight ►
White patch on
back, broad white
band on back of wing

BREEDING

WINTER

◄ Seasonal variation
Brownest and most heavily
spotted in summer, grey-brown in
winter; red on bill, bright vermilion
legs, white underwing

DISTRIBUTION
Widespread
breeder, but
declining inland;
in winter mostly
coastal, on estuaries
and floods

27–29cm 11in

IDENTIFICATION Noisy wader, often flying up with loud, hysterical calls, revealing broad white hindwing bands and white V on back. Legs vivid red. Darker, more spotted in summer; young birds paler, yellowish-brown, with more yellow-orange legs. Calls include ringing *teu-hu-hu* and *tewk-tewk-ew*. Loud, rhythmic song.

HABITAT Breeds on saltmarshes, damp pastures. In winter mostly on muddy estuaries, but some also on rocky shores, inland pools.

BEHAVIOUR Roosts in dense groups, but disperses to feed, scattered across mudflats or rocky foreshore, where it probes and delves for small animals, moving quite slowly.

▼ **Flight impressions**
Like miniature greenshank
with dark wings, white on
back and tail; long legs
project beyond tail tip

Marsh Sandpiper
Tringa stagnatilis

22–25cm 9–10in

DISTRIBUTION
Mostly a spring and
autumn migrant in
E Europe, rare and
erratic in west, on
coastal marshes,
inland lakes

▲ **Juvenile**
More buff-brown than
winter adult; needle-fine
bill, yellow-green legs

▲ **Adults**
Brown, spotted black, in spring (left),
greyer with white underside in
winter (right); dull greenish legs

IDENTIFICATION Much smaller than similar greenshank,
smaller and slighter than redshank; long, slender legs and very fine
bill. Dark wings, white V on lower back like greenshank in flight.
Needle-like, straight bill (and size if compared with other birds)
useful clues. Slimmer, taller than wood sandpiper, legs less yellow.
Call is sharp, high *kyew* or *kyew-kyew-kyew*.

HABITAT Mostly freshwater or brackish pools, muddy edges of
marshes and lakes, saline lagoons near the coast.

BEHAVIOUR A noticeably elegant, dainty wader, feeding at the
water's edge or wading in quite deeply to pick food from the surface
with its bill. Often with other waders, but rarely numerous.

Greenshank
Tringa nebularia

▼ Breeding adult
Greyish with bold marbling above, irregular blacker feathers; streaked neck and chest

▲ Autumn and winter
Pale greyish, often whiter on head and neck, white beneath; upcurved greyish bill; legs dull grey-green

Flight pattern ▲
Dark, with no wingbar, but long white V on back, pale tail; legs extend a little beyond tail tip

30–35cm 12–14in

DISTRIBUTION
Local breeder on moors, tundra; otherwise mostly freshwater, also saltmarsh and estuary creeks

IDENTIFICATION Medium-large wader: bigger, longer, longer-legged, and thicker-billed than redshank. Legs yellowish-green to dull grey-green. Looks greyer than most waders; often white streaks on head and neck coalescing into pale stripe on hindneck. Dark wings and white V on back make distinctive flight pattern. Call is more evenly paced than redshank's: a fluty *tew tew tew* or *chu-chu-chu*.

HABITAT Breeds on remote moors. Migrants often beside fresh waters, also on coasts; in winter on sheltered estuaries.

BEHAVIOUR Often alone or in small groups, feeding in shallow water, sometimes chasing prey, but often more sedate; a shy bird.

Green Sandpiper
Tringa ochropus

21–24cm 9–10in

DISTRIBUTION
Rare and local breeder in wet forest clearings; migrants beside freshwater and in estuary creeks

IDENTIFICATION Looks rather long and low, with medium-short bill and dull, medium-short legs. Dark above and on chest, white below. In flight, striking dark upperside and blackish underwing contrast with white belly and bold, square white rump and tail. Tail has few broad bars. Call is rich, yodelling *tluwee-wee-wee*.

HABITAT Shallow water and muddy edges of pools; narrow creeks, ditches, and streams.

BEHAVIOUR Feeds from mud or shallow water, but is so quick to take flight that it is more often seen flying away than feeding.

▼ Flight ▶
Dark wings above and below, white belly, square white rump (no V-shape)

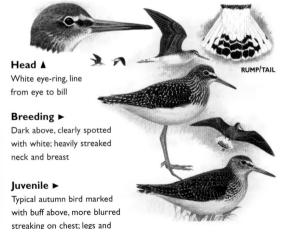

Head ▲
White eye-ring, line from eye to bill

RUMP/TAIL

Breeding ▶
Dark above, clearly spotted with white; heavily streaked neck and breast

Juvenile ▶
Typical autumn bird marked with buff above, more blurred streaking on chest; legs and base of bill dull grey-green

Wood Sandpiper
Tringa glareola

HEAD PATTERN

◄ Flight and tail
Underwing grey-buff, but
beware dark shadow; tail
barred, smaller white rump
than green sandpiper

DISTRIBUTION
Local breeder in
northern marshy
woods; migrant by
freshwater, including
coastal pools,
muddy marshes

19–21cm 8in

SUMMER ADULT

Flight ►
Dark, with small
square white
rump, dull tail;
feet project

◄ Autumn juvenile
Copious pale spots;
long stripe over eye;
long, yellow-ochre legs

JUVENILE

IDENTIFICATION Like green
sandpiper with longer legs; smaller than
redshank. Compared with green, has browner
back, larger pale spots above, and much longer pale line from bill
reaching well behind eye; also a smaller white rump, more heavily
barred tail, a paler underwing (which can look dark against sky),
longer, yellower legs, and a different call, a sharper *chiff-chiff-chiff*.
Not present in Europe in winter, unlike green sandpiper.

HABITAT Breeds in wet forest clearings, marshes. On migration,
beside fresh and brackish pools with mud and shallow water.

BEHAVIOUR Shy and easily disturbed, tending to fly off high,
with noisy calls. Bobs head and tail when nervous. Feeds by walking
over mud or in shallows, picking food from the surface with delicate
action. Usually seen in ones and twos, not larger flocks.

Common Sandpiper
Actitis hypoleucos

▼ Flight pattern
Stiff, broad wings have white stripe; round tail

▼ Juvenile
Very white below, white peak in front of wing; fine bars, pale notches on feather edges above

JUVENILE

▲ Adult
White underside curves up in front of wing; dull legs and bill

SUMMER ADULT

DISTRIBUTION
Common breeder by rivers and lakes; widespread migrant inland and on coasts, rare in winter

19–21cm 8in

IDENTIFICATION A small, neat, brown-and-white sandpiper with a white crescent or peak in front of closed wing, dull bill and leg colours, longish tail. Frequent quick bobbing of head and almost constant up–down swaying of rear body. Long, white wingbar obvious in flight. Loud, ringing calls, *tsweee-wee-wee,* and fast, trilling songs.

HABITAT Breeds on grassy and stony riverbanks or beside lakes in upland areas. On migration, by almost any freshwater and on rocky coasts, or in sheltered creeks; not open mudflats or estuaries.

BEHAVIOUR Usually in ones, twos, or threes, but occasionally 10 or more together on migration. Active on shore, walking quickly with distinctive bobbing motion; flies with stiff, bowed wings.

Red-necked Phalarope
Phalaropus lobatus

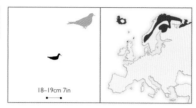

18–19cm 7in

DISTRIBUTION
Very local breeder beside lakes and marshes; migrants scarce, on sea or coastal pools; in winter out at sea

IDENTIFICATION A small, aquatic wader with a very fine needle bill, small head on rather long neck, broad body, and longish tail. Swims more than wades. In summer unmistakable, dark, with striped back, white throat, rust-red on neck. Juvenile striped black and buff, without clear grey areas on back shown by young grey phalarope. In winter has grey plumage with narrow, curved dark eye patch, like grey phalarope, but generally darker. Long white stripe on blackish wings, dark-centred rump, recalling sanderling. Thinner bill than grey phalarope with no yellow at base; blackish legs.

HABITAT Breeds by northern pools near marshy areas of tundra. Migrants may appear briefly on shallow coastal pools, rarely inland. Otherwise lives out at sea.

BEHAVIOUR Often wades around in shallows at edge of pool, but usually seen swimming, with head hunched or raised, foreparts of body higher than tail; may "spin" on one spot in characteristic way, stirring up food which it picks from the surface.

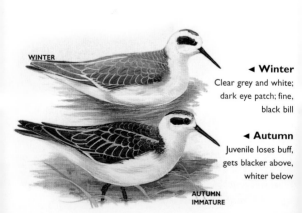

WINTER

◀ **Winter**
Clear grey and white; dark eye patch; fine, black bill

◀ **Autumn**
Juvenile loses buff, gets blacker above, whiter below

AUTUMN IMMATURE

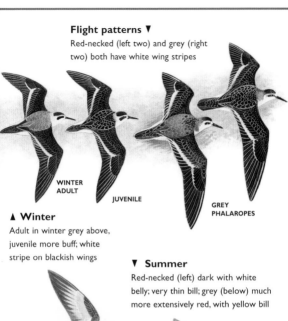

Flight patterns ▼
Red-necked (left two) and grey (right two) both have white wing stripes

WINTER ADULT

JUVENILE

GREY PHALAROPES

▲ Winter
Adult in winter grey above, juvenile more buff; white stripe on blackish wings

▼ Summer
Red-necked (left) dark with white belly; very thin bill; grey (below) much more extensively red, with yellow bill

Summer ▲
Dark marks on white underwing; grey flanks and white belly

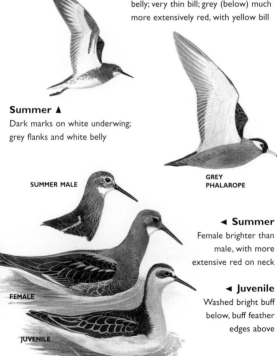

SUMMER MALE

GREY PHALAROPE

◄ Summer
Female brighter than male, with more extensive red on neck

◄ Juvenile
Washed bright buff below, buff feather edges above

FEMALE

JUVENILE

Grey Phalarope

*Phalaropus
fulicarius*

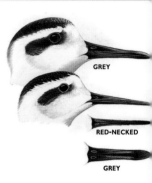

GREY

RED-NECKED

GREY

Head and bill ▶
Grey larger than red-necked;
bill thicker and broader, while
red-necked is needle-fine

20–22cm 8–9in

DISTRIBUTION
Breeds in Iceland;
widespread but
scarce migrant on
sea and coasts,
occasionally inland;
out at sea in winter

IDENTIFICATION Typical phalarope, with thin bill, wide body, shortish legs. Usually seen swimming, with head held well up, but may be more hunched, especially if exhausted in rough weather. In summer easy to tell by bold rufous plumage, black cap, white on face, yellow on bill. Autumn birds more like red-necked, but have more clear, pale grey on back (no bright buff stripes on juvenile, but rounded spots of grey and bands of blackish-brown). Has thicker bill, often with touch of yellow at base; tends to have wider, less curved black patch behind eye. Call is sharp, metallic *pit*. Swimming winter spotted redshank much bigger, longer-billed; sanderling lacks eye patch, runs on beaches, and rarely swims.

HABITAT Breeds near northern lakes in tundra or open moorland. Migrants occasionally on inland pools, more often on coastal lagoons, but mostly on the sea, most often seen from land during gales.

BEHAVIOUR Phalaropes do walk along shores, with a rather clumsy gait; also wade, but are far more often seen swimming, much more persistently than other waders. Their ability to spend months on the sea, far from land, is remarkable, especially considering their small size. On the water, grey phalaropes may be seen in small groups, swimming buoyantly, their foreparts higher than their tapered tails, looking very pale grey and white, like minute gulls.

▼ Summer
Male (left) duller than female (below); female rich red, with bold white face

JUVENILE

AUTUMN IMMATURE

Autumn ▲
Juvenile rapidly loses buff, becoming grey and white with worn blackish feathers on back and wings, less striped than red-necked

Autumn and winter ▼
Dark summer feathers gradually replaced by pale grey above, pure white below

On water ▶
Swims buoyantly; looks very pale and very small when seen on open sea

Turnstone
Arenaria interpres

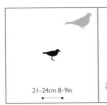

21–24cm 8–9in

DISTRIBUTION
A northern breeding bird, on islands and tundra; widespread on coasts for most of year, scarce inland

▼ Winter
Stocky, short-billed, with short, thick, dark bill, short, bright orange legs, dark, mottled upperparts, and strikingly bright, white underside; curved black breastband

WINTER

Autumn juvenile ▼
Like winter adult, but a little paler, with fine buff edges to upperpart feathers, more diffuse face pattern

▲ Winter group
Feeds on seaweed-covered rocks, weedy shores of sand and gravel

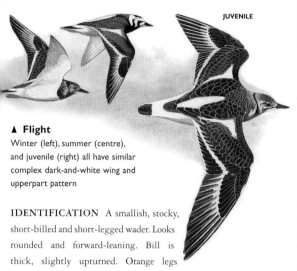

JUVENILE

▲ Flight
Winter (left), summer (centre), and juvenile (right) all have similar complex dark-and-white wing and upperpart pattern

IDENTIFICATION A smallish, stocky, short-billed and short-legged wader. Looks rounded and forward-leaning. Bill is thick, slightly upturned. Orange legs distinctive. In winter dark above, with pale marks on face and broad, curved blackish band on chest; clear white beneath. In summer upperparts marked with rich rusty-red and black, head black and white. In flight very dark, marked by complex "flickering" pattern of white on wings, back, and rump. Calls include quick, rattling, or staccato *kitikikikik*, *tuk-a-tuk* and *tit-tit* notes.

HABITAT Breeds on coastal tundra and rocky islands. Migrants and wintering birds prefer shingly or sandy shores, rocky beaches with plentiful seaweed, and the vicinity of piers, groynes, and promenades. Some appear beside reservoirs inland on migration.

BEHAVIOUR A busy, social, noisy bird, feeding on weedy rocks at the edge of the sea, darting about to avoid incoming waves or to find new feeding areas, often in flocks of around 10 or 20. Larger numbers gather to roost at high tide, frequently with other waders such as dunlins and ringed plovers. Turnstones are inquisitive and opportunistic feeders, searching under weed and tipping over small stones and shells to disturb minute aquatic invertebrates.

◀ Summer
Beautiful rich chestnut-red-, black--and-white pattern, unique and unmistakable; leans forward to pick food from ground

Pomarine Skua
Stercorarius pomarinus

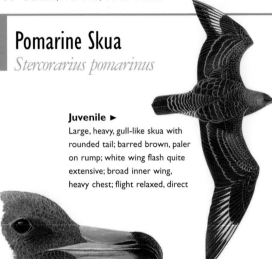

Juvenile ▶
Large, heavy, gull-like skua with rounded tail; barred brown, paler on rump; white wing flash quite extensive; broad inner wing, heavy chest; flight relaxed, direct

◄ Juvenile
Thick bill pale (blue-grey) at base, black at tip, visible at long range

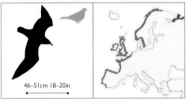

46–51cm 18–20in

DISTRIBUTION
Northern breeder on moors, tundra; migrants at sea and inshore, especially off headlands, in spring and autumn

IDENTIFICATION A large skua, bigger than common gull, smaller than herring gull; heavier, deeper-bellied, thicker-billed than Arctic skua. Spring adult obvious owing to long, blunt tail projection; more difficult if projection is lost through moult or broken off. Juvenile usually dark, with head and belly as dark as rest (often paler on Arctic); tail rounded, then with blunt (not sharp) central projection. Steady, direct flight useful clue at all ages.

HABITAT Breeds on tundra; rest of year spent at sea, often close inshore on migration, rarely in winter.

BEHAVIOUR A predator of small mammals and birds in summer, but mostly piratical at other times, chasing large terns and gulls to steal their fish. Acrobatic and fast in the chase; more regular normal flight lacks jerky effect of Arctic skua, or power of great skua.

▼ Pale adult
Double pale patch beneath wing; dark cap, pale underside, dark breastband; heavy impression

▲ Juvenile below
Large pale wing flash, often with small pale inner crescent on primary coverts

▲ Juvenile
Greyish underwing with "double" pale patch towards tip; heavy, flattish belly

◄ Tail shapes
Rounded on juvenile (top); with age becomes wedge-shaped with blunt central projection (lower); adult has long, blunt, twisted projection

▼ Juvenile
More rufous form; some look much darker overall

▼ Adults
Pale form; some uniformly dark except for extensive pale wing patches; tail projection blunt, "spoon-shaped" on older birds

Arctic Skua
Stercorarius parasiticus

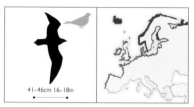

41–46cm 16–18in

DISTRIBUTION
Local breeder on
moorland and
islands; widespread
off coasts in spring
and autumn,
rare winter

▼ **Pale adult**
Dark above, whitish below, with
soft, dusky breastband (coarser,
barred on pomarine); black cap

▼ **Immature**
Often rufous, or greyer with paler
belly; marked white wing flash;
develops adult features with age

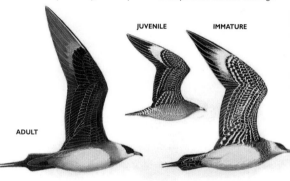

JUVENILE

IMMATURE

ADULT

IDENTIFICATION About kittiwake-sized, light, quick, elegant
in flight; usually the commonest skua. Adults dark brown type; pale
type with darker cap and paler underside; or intermediate with dark
cap, grey brown above, and creamy below with darker wash across
chest. Juveniles bright rufous-brown or sandy, with darker flight
feathers, pale bars above and below tail, and small whitish wing
flashes; often paler on head and belly. Tail projection short, pointed
on immatures; longer, thin, and spike-like on adults. Bill fairly
slender; pale base on juvenile not obvious at long range.

HABITAT Breeds on moors and islands. Otherwise at sea, often
close inshore, even in estuaries on migration.

BEHAVIOUR Piratical, chasing terns and small gulls, often with
fast, acrobatic, determined chase by one or two birds. On migration
tends to fly by low over sea, often changing height and direction.

▲ Pale adults
Dark cap, pale chest and
belly; commoner than
dark type in far north

Bill ▲
Bill slimmer than pomarine
and long-tailed skuas

Juvenile ►
Dark form, with white flash
on wing; short tail projection
becomes longer with age

Juvenile ►
Tends to look dark and rufous
or yellowish-brown; rump quite
dark, head rufous; more white in
wing than on long-tailed skua

Dark adult ▲
Commoner than pale form
in southern parts of range

Juvenile ▲ ►
Short, pointed
tail projection

Long-tailed Skua
Stercorarius longicaudus

JUVENILES

JUVENILE TAIL

◄ **Bill detail**
Short but thick bill

◄ **Juvenile**
All-dark or pale, greyish, with paler head, pale belly

Adult ►
Whippy tail projection; dark wing; pale chest, dusky belly

◄ **Juveniles**
Dark trailing edge to wing; paler underside

48–53cm 19–21in

DISTRIBUTION
Local breeder on tundra; widespread on migration, but usually scarce off western coasts

IDENTIFICATION Smallest, lightest, most tern-like skua, but deep-chested effect in flight. Adult pale on chest with no breastband, but dusky on belly and dark under tail; neat black cap, minimal white wing flash; dark flight feathers contrast with paler upperwing; long, flexible tail spike. Juvenile slender-winged, with small, rounded tail projection; some are all-dark, but most are pale, greyish, with light head and whitish belly, boldly barred under tail.

HABITAT Breeds on tundra, high moors above tree line. Migrants at sea or in inshore waters, occasionally coming to rest on land.

BEHAVIOUR Predatory and piratical, but catches more fish directly than other skuas. A graceful, elegant skua, swimming buoyantly with tail raised clear of water.

Great Skua
Stercorarius skua

◄ Flight from below
Big, dark or rusty-brown,
with large and striking white
wing patches; broad but
pointed wings

◄ Adult from above
Heavy, brown skua with short,
square or wedge-shaped tail
with minute projection; big
white flash on broad wings

53–64cm 21–25in

DISTRIBUTION
Local breeder on
northern islands
and moors;
widespread off
coasts in spring
and autumn

IDENTIFICATION The biggest skua, looking especially heavy
in the body and broad-winged; head and bill powerful on ground,
but can look rather small in flight. Tail short, wide, with slight
central point. Looks warm, mid-brown with darker cap and flight
feathers. Large white patch beyond bend of wing, especially beneath,
bigger than on other skuas. Paler hackles on neck may give golden-
brown appearance in summer when feathers fade paler.

HABITAT Breeds on heathery moors and islands; otherwise at sea,
but often close inshore on migration.

BEHAVIOUR Bold, aggressive,
a predator on seabirds at all times,
as well as a pirate, chasing birds as
large as gannets to steal food.

THICK BILL

▲ Size comparison
Arctic (left), pomarine (centre), and
much bigger great skua (right)

Mediterranean Gull
Larus melanocephalus

36–38cm 14–15in

DISTRIBUTION
Extremely local breeder; widespread from late spring to late winter, on beaches, estuaries, nearby fields

IDENTIFICATION About black-headed gull size, but stockier, with larger head, stouter bill, slightly broader wings, stiffer flight. Adult has wholly white underwings, frosty grey upperwings fading to whitish tips; legs and bill vary from red to blackish. In summer has jet-black hood, white eyelids, scarlet bill. Juvenile heavily mottled above. First winter pale grey on back, pale midwing panel, dark trailing edge, and blackish wingtips; smudge or "pirate patch" through eye. Looks more like black-headed gull on ground, but like young common gull in flight. Two-year-old like adult, but has small, sharp, black marks on wingtip.

HABITAT Coastal lakes, beaches, coasts including harbours, piers.

BEHAVIOUR Similar to black-headed gull, but often bold and more aggressive in character. Often with flocks of other gulls.

First year ▼
Dark smudge behind eye curves up over nape; white eyelids; dark wingtip and tailband; bill all-dark or buff-orange at base; legs orange, red, or black

JUVENILE

Adult ▼
All-white wingtip eyecatching

MALE

FEMALE

WINTER ADULT

SUMMER ADULT

First winter ►
Pale grey back and midwing
panel; forewing brown, fades
paler in spring; outer wing
black-brown, fades browner;
pale lines on inner edge of
wingtip feathers visible when
spread, unlike common gull

Tail length ▼
Female's tail (lower) shorter
than male's

FEMALE

FIRST
WINTER

SECOND
WINTER

SUMMER
ADULT

FIRST WINTER

▲ Flight patterns
Like common gull in first year; develops
through pale second year with wingtip
spots to all-pale wing of adult; wing of
adult strikingly white beneath

Second year ►
Variable black bands
on wingtips; otherwise
as adult with red,
black, or orange legs,
red-and-black bill

Little Gull

Larus minutus

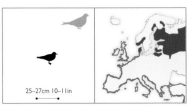

25–27cm 10–11in

DISTRIBUTION
Very local breeder
on floods, marshes;
widespread migrant
on coasts and
inland lakes, more
local in winter

▼ **Summer adult**
Small, neat gull with jet-black hood (no white
eyelids), pale back, white wingtips at rest
(dark on underwing may show)

Winter ▼
Grey cap and ear
spot, fine black bill

SECOND YEAR

First winter ▲
Dark juvenile upperparts
gradually become pale grey, but in autumn
dusky breast patch and collar remain

JUVENILE

IDENTIFICATION Smallest gull, tern-like, but adults have broader, rounder wings. Very short legs; short, fine bill. Adult has all-pale upperwing, with white band around hind edge to tip; underwing blackish, with white trailing edge. Head black in summer, bill dark red, legs red. In winter bill black, head white with grey marks near eye. Juvenile barred dark brown above; first winter gets grey back (with dusky collar and lower back at first), but wings have black W effect with diagonal band across coverts and dark outer primaries, striped white when spread. Young kittiwake much bigger, always grey on back, collar narrower and blacker, never dark on lower back, outer primaries more solidly black. Two-year-old like

▼ First summer
Gains variable dark hood; dark zigzag
and wing fades browner.

First winter ►
Dark back of juvenile
replaced by pale grey
(initially with dark collar and
rump remaining); pale, with
black W on wing. White
streaks on wingtip.

FIRST WINTER

FIRST SUMMER

WINTER
ADULT

SECOND
WINTER

FIRST WINTER

◄ Adult
Very pale in winter,
with white line around
upperwing, but underwing
sooty-black with white trailing edge
and tip. Black hood in summer

SECOND
SUMMER

SUMMER ADULT

adult, but wingtips marked with black, underwing dusky grey.
Complex transitions between plumages, but always small, delicate,
feeding by dipping to surface of water.

HABITAT Breeds on wet marshes inland. Migrants follow coasts
and appear at inland lakes and reservoirs, often moving through
quickly. In winter on coasts and also out at sea.

BEHAVIOUR Usually in small groups of up to 20 or so, but may
congregate in larger flocks. Often seen with much larger numbers of
black-headed gulls, or resting with gulls and terns. Dainty, buoyant,
floating over the water or flying with shallow wingbeats,
sideslipping or dipping down in a way that recalls black tern.

Black-headed Gull
Larus ridibundus

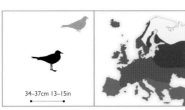

34–37cm 13–15in

DISTRIBUTION
Widespread
breeder on pools,
marshes, moors;
at other times
common almost
everywhere

IDENTIFICATION Small, very pale, fine-billed gull; underwing grey towards tip, but with white outer edge; upperwing has similar white flash on fore edge, narrow black trailing edge at tip. Adult has brown hood in summer, white head with dark ear spot in winter, red legs. Juvenile marked with pale brown, legs paler, similar white flash on wing, but paler grey underwing. Loud, squealing, laughing calls.

HABITAT Breeds on peaty pools on moors, near reedbeds, on floods, and on saltmarshes. At other times almost any open ground, from town centres to tops of hills, especially near rivers and lakes, and on all kinds of coasts, except sheer cliffs and rocky islands.

BEHAVIOUR A lively, noisy bird, always in groups, gathering in large flocks where food is abundant (as on tips, or at outflows over beaches) or to roost (on reservoirs or the sea). Flight is light and easy, with quick wingbeats; gives flickering effect at long range.

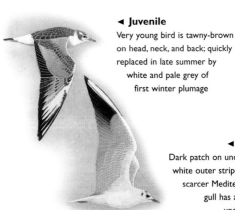

◄ Juvenile
Very young bird is tawny-brown
on head, neck, and back; quickly
replaced in late summer by
white and pale grey of
first winter plumage

◄ Adult
Dark patch on underwing,
white outer stripe (much
scarcer Mediterranean
gull has all-white
underwing)

WINTER

SUMMER

FIRST
WINTER

▲ Flight
Upperwing (top) has bold white flash on outer edge, thin black trailing edge; underwing dark towards tip

On ground ▲
Very pale grey and white; summer adult has brown hood, tilted forward, dark red bill and legs; winter adult has brighter bill and legs, white head with dark spot; first year marked with brown on wings, paler legs and bill

First year ►
Dark trailing edge; brown diagonal band; white flash on outer wing partially obscured by dark marks, which wear off by summer

Winter adult ▼
Very clean and bright, with distinctive white wing flash, white head

Longer tail of male outlined (left)

FIRST SUMMER

FIRST WINTER

ADULT

Slender-billed Gull
Larus genei

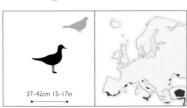

37–42cm 15–17in

DISTRIBUTION
Extremely local breeder; at other times more widespread, mostly on Mediterranean coasts

▼ **Flight**
Like black-headed, but all-white head; long neck, heavy body, broader wings

▼ **On ground**
Longish bill, red or black; faint dusky cheek spot in winter; white head in summer; long body

BLACK-HEADED GULL

WINTER

SUMMER

JUVENILE

FIRST WINTER

IDENTIFICATION Like a black-headed gull with a white head; slightly larger, with broader wing, longer body, shorter wingtip at rest. Forehead slopes forward in "snout" effect; neck long when extended. In flight head protrudes more, tail slightly longer; deeper, flatter belly profile. Adult's pale eye hard to see; bill deep red or black in summer, orange-red in winter. Juvenile has paler wing markings than black-headed, and paler bill.

HABITAT Breeds on saltmarshes and lagoons near coast. At other times occurs in sandy bays, on sandy beaches, and on coastal pools.

BEHAVIOUR Much the same as other small gulls; often swims on pools or sea in small groups. Generally a scarce bird.

Audouin's Gull
Larus audouinii

44–52cm 17–20in

DISTRIBUTION
Almost entirely
Mediterranean,
breeding on islands
and east coast of
Spain, wandering
more in winter

IDENTIFICATION Like herring gull at long range, but wedge of black at wingtip, narrow wings, and long, white head and neck create more gannet-like look in flight. Bill looks thick, blunt, and dark; eye very dark. Close to, red bill, elongated forehead, faintly grey body, and dark grey legs all help identify adults and immatures. Juvenile like small, dark herring gull with long wingtips, plain brown chest, boldly marked underwing; thick, dark bill with dull pale base.

HABITAT Breeds on rocky islands and sandbars; otherwise offshore or on sandy beaches and outlets of rivers.

BEHAVIOUR Mostly marine, catching fish from surface while in flight, but also rests on lagoons, and sandy or rocky shores.

▼ Immatures
Juvenile (left) has solidly dark tail, white rump,
dark wings; well-marked underwing; develops
grey back with age

JUVENILES

ADULTS

ADULT

▲ At rest
Juvenile (above) dark, scaly;
adult pale; head white, underside
pale grey; grey legs; dark eye

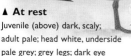

JUVENILE

Flight ▲
Adult silver-grey with
black wingtip wedge;
white spots at tip
wear off in summer

Common Gull
Larus canus

38–44cm 15–17in

DISTRIBUTION
Local breeder on coasts and moors; in autumn to spring widespread inland and on coast, but still localized

▼ Second year
Like adult, but wingtip solidly dark; often dark band or tip to bill; dull legs; head closely streaked grey-brown in winter

IDENTIFICATION Medium-small gull, bigger than black-headed, smaller than herring, but similar pattern. Flight buoyant and fluent, soars less than herring gull. Adult has smaller head, finer bill with no red spot, dark eye, greenish legs. Large black wingtip with bold white spots. Second year has more black on outer wing, smaller white spots. Juvenile and first year brown on wings, with paler midwing, dark trailing edge, and blackish wedge at tip; neat, sharp black band on tail unlike herring gull. Pattern like young Mediterranean, but less contrasted (in summer, darker grey back creates "saddle" against pale wings, unlike paler Mediterranean).

HABITAT Breeds on heather moors near sea, coastal rocks, and small islands. At other times on beaches, estuaries, fields, floods.

BEHAVIOUR Less aggressive than herring gull. Likes grassy areas or beaches, walking in search of food. Often hundreds or thousands where common, but in many areas less abundant than other gulls.

▼ Flight patterns

Juvenile has darker midwing than Mediterranean gull; sharper tailband than herring gull

SUMMER ADULT

JUVENILE

FIRST YEAR

ADULT UNDERWING

SECOND YEAR

▼ Adult

Grey above, darker than British herring gull, with larger white patch between back and wingtip; small, greenish bill; green legs; dark eye; head streaked in winter

WINTER ADULT

SUMMER ADULT

First year ▲

Grey back, browner wings (fade to buff in summer) with blackish tips; orange-buff bill with black tip; buff-pink legs

FIRST WINTER

Lesser Black-backed Gull
Larus fuscus

52–67cm 21–26in

DISTRIBUTION
Local breeder in north-west; widespread on coasts and inland lakes in autumn, fewer in winter

IDENTIFICATION Large gull, white-headed in summer, streaked in winter; darker than herring or yellow-legged, paler than great black-backed (except NW European races, which are equally black). Yellow legs distinctive. Adult has less white on wingtip, smaller bill than larger great black-backed. Juvenile darker than herring with more uniform wing; gains dark grey back with age. SW Scandinavian/Low Countries race blacker than UK/Iceland birds; Baltic race longer-winged, jet-black above, white-headed in winter.

HABITAT Breeds on cliffs, islands, and moors; at other times on coasts, inland waters, rubbish tips, fields, in harbours, or out at sea.

BEHAVIOUR Aggressive predator in summer, although Baltic race eats more fish. Colonial breeder, usually in flocks.

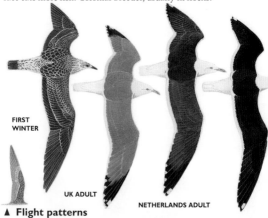

FIRST WINTER

UK ADULT

NETHERLANDS ADULT

BALTIC

▲ Flight patterns
First year wing all-dark; UK adult slate-grey with blacker wingtips, Netherlands/SW Scandinavian race (or species) darker, Baltic race black, slim-winged

Juvenile ►
During first year, wings dark; whole outer wing blackish (paler behind angle on herring gull); dark coverts (paler on herring, contrasting more with dark trailing edge)

Adult from below ►
Darker grey flight feathers than herring gull

BALTIC

NETHERLANDS

UK SUMMER

Racial variation ▲
Baltic race (or species) very black, head white all year; W European race intermediate; UK race paler; all have bright yellow legs

JUVENILE

Herring Gull
Larus argentatus

55–67cm 22–26in

DISTRIBUTION
Widespread, inland mostly in winter; yellow-legged birds in Mediterranean, move north in late summer/autumn

Juveniles ▼
Dark brown; tertials (between back and wingtip) have pale notches along edges (on lesser black-backed more solid brown); bill develops paler base with age

Adults ▼
Scandinavian birds (upper) big, darker above, often less black on wingtip than UK/Iceland/ W European ones (lower)

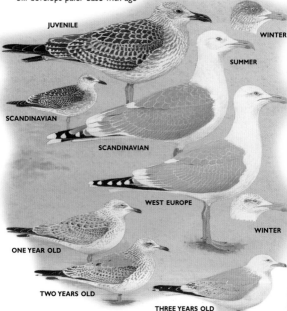

JUVENILE

WINTER

SUMMER

SCANDINAVIAN

SCANDINAVIAN

WEST EUROPE

WINTER

ONE YEAR OLD

TWO YEARS OLD

THREE YEARS OLD

Immaturity ▲
Easier to tell from lesser black-backed gull with increasing age as paler grey back becomes obvious; rate of change variable

▲ Seasonal change
Head and neck pure white from about February to August; at other times variable grey-brown streaks and mottling

Yellow-legged gull ▼

Juveniles dark rusty-brown; whiter head, black bill; adult dark, white head except late summer, bright yellow legs

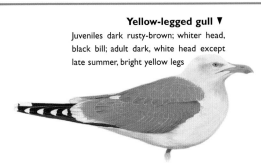

IDENTIFICATION Large, grey-backed gull, white head streaked in winter. Darker grey in Scandinavia (pink legs) and Mediterranean (yellow legs). Black wingtips spotted white; yellow bill with red spot; pale eyes (common gull has green legs, dark eyes, no red on bill). Juvenile paler than lesser black-backed, paler patch behind bend of wing. Immatures get pale grey on back, paler than lesser black-backed; bigger than common, with less well defined tailband. Mediterranean adults whiter-headed in winter, legs bright yellow; immatures more rufous, darker tailband; probably a separate species.

HABITAT Coasts of all kinds, inland waters, fields, tips.

BEHAVIOUR Noisy, bold, and aggressive; breeds in colonies; usually seen in flocks or with other gulls. The typical silver-backed "seaside" gull of promenades, piers, and rooftops.

▼ Flight

Pale grey contrasts with dark wingtip more than on darker lesser black-backed; paler underwing; Scandinavian darker, less black, more white, some almost no black under wingtip

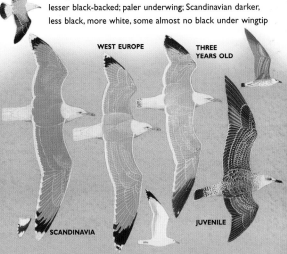

WEST EUROPE

THREE YEARS OLD

SCANDINAVIA

JUVENILE

Iceland Gull
Larus glaucoides

52–60cm 21–24in

DISTRIBUTION
Breeds Greenland/
Canada; scarce in
winter, in harbours,
on inland waters,
around trawlers, in
varying numbers

IDENTIFICATION A large, pale gull, forming a difficult pair with glaucous gull, with almost identical plumage patterns. Adult told from herring gull by more white and lack of black on wingtips; immatures have no dark trailing edge to wing, or tailband. Compared to glaucous, adult has shorter bill, usually steeper forehead, and more gentle expression, longer wingtip extending farther beyond tail, shorter legs. Immatures identified by same structural features; first year has particularly long, pointed wingtip at rest, angled up when on water; bill darker, with more black at tip, duller base (pink with sharp black tip on first-year glaucous), but in later years of immaturity bill becomes paler with smaller dark band at tip. Beware small glaucous gulls, which can be told with difficulty by shorter wingtip projection and fiercer look about the head.

HABITAT Usually seen in winter in vicinity of harbours, especially fish quays, and also on inland waters; usually in ones and twos, with larger flocks of herring gulls.

BEHAVIOUR Usually a rather sluggish gull, spending much time doing very little, resting on beach or in vicinity of rubbish tip, but can be aggressive when feeding.

First winter ▲
Compare head and bill with glaucous; plumage similar, but longer wingtips (all pale), shorter legs

▲ Bill
Dark tip extends back as wedge unlike glaucous, less with age

Flight silhouette ▶
Iceland (upper) lighter than glaucous (lower), but still round-bodied; long wings narrower at tip than glaucous

◀ First year
Pale oatmeal-cream overall, fades even paler in summer; no dark hindwing or tailband, no dark brown on wingtip

GLAUCOUS

▲ Adult
Pattern as glaucous or with slightly sharper contrast between grey and white of wingtip; broad white trailing edge

WINTER ADULT

SECOND YEAR

Age variation ▲
Adult has long, white wingtips, dusky head in winter, deep pink legs, beady eye; first year fades whiter

FIRST SUMMER

Glaucous Gull
Larus hyperboreus

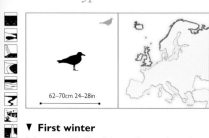

62–70cm 24–28in

DISTRIBUTION
Local breeder in
Iceland; widespread
but very scarce on
NW European
coasts, winter and
early spring

▼ **First winter**
Pale oatmeal-buff with brown bars and mottles,
often darker below; short wingtip
projection; pink bill with
black tip

ADULT SUMMER

IDENTIFICATION A big gull, between herring gull and great black-backed, but often slimmer-billed than latter. Despite size, can be an elegant bird; head can be round, but typically less dove-like than Iceland gull, with longer bill. Wingtip projects less beyond tip of tail than on Iceland. Wingtips and underwing always very pale, white on adult, ivory to buff on immature, striking when settled and especially in flight (wingtips darker than back on herring gull). Bill colour on first year cleaner, pinker, with less black on tip than on first year Iceland, but older Icelands look more similar. Small glaucous gull can be difficult to distinguish from larger Icelands at times.

HABITAT Rocky shores, quays, beaches of all kinds; also regular but rare on reservoirs and rubbish tips inland.

BEHAVIOUR A big, aggressive gull, dominating smaller species. Typically spends much time "doing nothing" on beach or swimming, usually with other gulls; feeds at tips, sewage and other outflows, and along the water's edge, looking for fish and refuse.

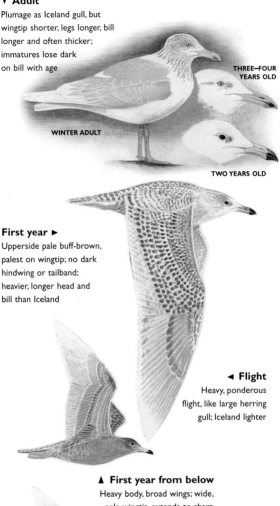

▼ Adult
Plumage as Iceland gull, but wingtip shorter, legs longer, bill longer and often thicker; immatures lose dark on bill with age

THREE–FOUR YEARS OLD

WINTER ADULT

TWO YEARS OLD

First year ▶
Upperside pale buff-brown, palest on wingtip; no dark hindwing or tailband; heavier, longer head and bill than Iceland

◀ Flight
Heavy, ponderous flight, like large herring gull; Iceland lighter

▲ First year from below
Heavy body, broad wings; wide, pale wingtip extends to sharp point (blunter on older birds)

◀ Iceland gull comparison
Slightly smaller, body quite rounded, wings broad-based, but longer, more tapered than glaucous; bill dark

Great Black-backed Gull
Larus marinus

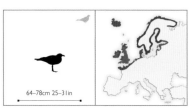

64–78cm 25–31in

DISTRIBUTION
Local breeder on cliffs; from autumn to spring more widespread on beaches and locally inland

IDENTIFICATION The largest of the gulls: heavily built, with a specially thick, heavy bill, and a large, rounded head. Adult black above, white below; more white on wingtip, less streaked on head in winter than lesser black-backed gull. Legs pale pink to greyish, not yellow. Immature gains black patches above with age, so becomes more easily identifiable, but first year pale, more boldly chequered

▼ Variation with age
Pale and boldly chequered in first year; gains black on back and inner wing, then over whole upperside with increasing age

FIRST YEAR

TWO YEARS OLD

THIRD WINTER

SUMMER ADULT

WINTER ADULT

THREE–FOUR YEARS OLD

above than herring gull or lesser black-backed gull. Big, dark bill is a useful clue, contrasting with pale head and neck. In flight, juvenile and first-year birds have large whitish rump, narrow black tailband, large pale area behind bend of wing, whitish head; at this age more like a big, heavily marked herring gull than a lesser black-backed. Calls are mostly short, deep, and throaty.

HABITAT Breeds high up on cliffs, tops of offshore stacks, and islands; at other times on estuaries, beaches, lakes, and reservoirs, or out at sea among trawlers or following ships. Also on fields and even open moorland close to the coast.

BEHAVIOUR An aggressive predator, capable of killing smaller seabirds, ducks, and coots; despite this often rests quietly among other gulls, wildfowl, and waders. Also eats fish and refuse of all descriptions. Usually social, but typically in small numbers, scattered through larger flocks of other gulls; can form flocks of several hundreds where common.

▼ **Immatures in flight**
Whitish head and rump, narrow tailband; pale area on outer wing; gradually gains black above

▼ **Flight**
Third/fourth year, almost as adult, but with mottled wings, faint dark tail spots; adult black with big white wingtip spots

TWO YEARS OLD

THREE YEARS OLD

FIRST YEAR

▲ **Adult**
Very large, wings long and bowed, black above, dark beneath flight feathers

Kittiwake
Larus tridactyla

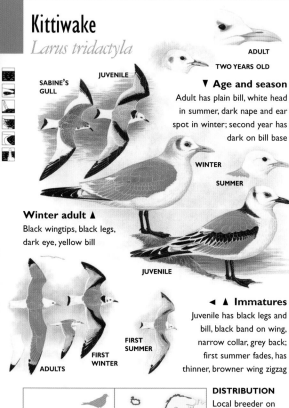

ADULT

TWO YEARS OLD

▼ Age and season
Adult has plain bill, white head in summer, dark nape and ear spot in winter; second year has dark on bill base

SABINE'S GULL

JUVENILE

WINTER

SUMMER

Winter adult ▲
Black wingtips, black legs, dark eye, yellow bill

JUVENILE

◄ ▲ Immatures
Juvenile has black legs and bill, black band on wing, narrow collar, grey back; first summer fades, has thinner, browner wing zigzag

FIRST SUMMER

FIRST WINTER

ADULTS

DISTRIBUTION
Local breeder on coastal cliffs; much more widely seen off coasts during rest of year

38–40cm 15–16in

IDENTIFICATION Medium-small gull; flies over sea, banking steeply like shearwater in wind. Pale grey; paler than back towards wingtip, which has black triangle without white spots. Legs short and blackish; bill greenish-yellow, red inside mouth, but no red spot. Juvenile has black zigzag above, like smaller little gull, but cleaner grey back, sharper black collar. Calls nasal *kiti-a-wa-ake* at colony.

HABITAT Breeds on sheer sea cliffs, sometimes buildings; otherwise at sea, but also in harbours. Rests on beaches in summer.

BEHAVIOUR Breeds in tight colonies, feeds out at sea.

Sabine's Gull
Larus sabini

27–32cm 11–13in

DISTRIBUTION
Arctic breeder;
small numbers
migrate south in
autumn along W
European coasts,
inshore in gales

IDENTIFICATION A small, elegant, long-winged gull with a three-triangle upperwing pattern, much sharper than faded immature kittiwakes with reduced zigzag pattern. No black between dark forewing and white hindwing. Adult lead-grey above, head grey in summer, white with dusky patch in winter; wingtip black with large white spot at tip of each feather. Juvenile/first year, as seen in autumn, scaly brown above, wingtip brownish-black, head brown at first, sides of neck and breast grey-brown, but striking wing pattern still obvious. Underwing white with dusky central line and dark tip. Flight light, easy, tern-like.

HABITAT Breeds in Arctic tundra. Migrates south in autumn through eastern Atlantic, usually well offshore, but variable numbers come close inshore in rough weather. Sometimes scores of hundreds seen off Ireland, SW Britain, NW France; regular but rare in North Sea. Much rarer in spring and summer, on beaches or offshore.

BEHAVIOUR Feeds by dipping to the surface, like a black tern, or picking food from the water while swimming. Usually with other gulls; rarely more than two or three Sabine's seen together in Europe.

Flight pattern ▶
Juvenile and adult share triple-triangle pattern, dark inner wing, black outer wing, white rear, no diagonal band

JUVENILE

Gull-billed Tern
Sterna nilotica

▼ Adults
Pale grey, white below; rump very pale grey; thick, black bill; black cap in summer, dark eye patch in winter

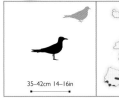

◄ Immature
Dusky eye patch; short, black bill; upperside mottled pale grey, faint darker hindwing band

35–42cm 14–16in

DISTRIBUTION
Extremely local on coasts, freshwater marshes; only a little more widely seen on migration

IDENTIFICATION Rather like a Sandwich tern in size and bulk, but bill always a little shorter, less tapered, all-black with no trace of any other colour. In summer, black cap is round and neat, not crested. In winter a very pale bird, pale grey rump hard to detect, head white with short blackish or grey patch behind eye. Juvenile more buffish above, but plainer above than young Sandwich tern, with shorter bill and rather long legs, obvious at rest. Harsh *gu-wick* call.

HABITAT Breeds on lakes, marshes, near floods and wet pastures; feeds over land more than water; also on beaches; migrates over the sea.

▼ Adult
Round black cap; shortish black bill; black legs

BEHAVIOUR More like whiskered tern than Sandwich tern, flying over shallow lagoons, wet grassy areas, and rice paddies, dipping down for food.

Little Tern
Sterna albifrons

22–24cm 9in

DISTRIBUTION
Local and declining
breeder, mostly on
coasts; more
widespread as
a migrant on
beaches, estuaries

IDENTIFICATION   Small, dumpy tern with long, tapered, pointed wings, longish, spike-like yellow bill, and short orange-yellow legs. Always has white forehead, neat black eye stripe and cap. Adult pale grey above, white on tail and below; looks very pale, apart from black outermost feathers of wing. Immature mottled grey-brown above, bill darker. Fast flight action distinctive, especially in hover before vertical dive. Rapid, chattering calls and rasping *kree-ek*.

HABITAT   Sand and shingle beaches; sometimes lagoons, estuaries.

BEHAVIOUR   Breeds in small colonies, where its noisy, hyperactive behaviour draws attention. Dives for fish with a loud "smack", often very close to the beach.

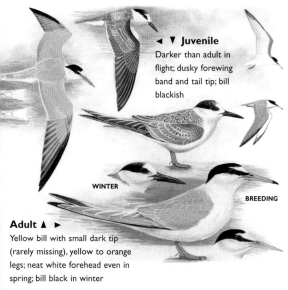

◄ ▼ Juvenile
Darker than adult in
flight; dusky forewing
band and tail tip; bill
blackish

WINTER

BREEDING

Adult ▲ ►
Yellow bill with small dark tip
(rarely missing), yellow to orange
legs; neat white forehead even in
spring; bill black in winter

Caspian Tern
Sterna caspia

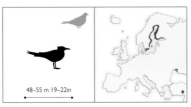

48–55 m 19–22in

DISTRIBUTION
Very localized
breeder on sand
or rocky beach;
rare migrant in S
and W Europe in
spring and autumn

IDENTIFICATION A very large tern, bigger than common gull, with a massive, blood-red bill (which looks enormous at close range, but not grotesquely so, and not over-striking in flight at a distance). Blackish underside to wingtip is eyecatching in flight, unlike any other red-billed tern. Black cap neat in summer (but straggly and crested at rear when raised); replaced by heavily streaked, less well defined cap in winter, without white forehead. Flight quite slow, front-heavy; dives with big splash. Loud, heron-like *kree-ahk* call.

HABITAT Breeds on low islands, sand bars, rocks. Seen more widely on migration, on lagoons near the coast or over the sea.

BEHAVIOUR A social tern, breeding in colonies, occasionally isolated pairs, and often resting with other terns and gulls on beaches. Feeds over open water, both salt and fresh, often very far from the colony.

▼ Juvenile
Mottled grey-brown above, with
dark wingtips and tail; crown closely
streaked; orange bill

◄ First year
White tail has dark
tip; cap like adult in
winter, closely
streaked with white

Flight from above ▶
Very big, gull-like tern, with
prominent head and bill; large bill
not always obvious at long range;
white rump and short white tail

◀ From below
Very white tern, with big
but not disproportionate
red bill; blackish under
wingtip giving distinctive
gannet-like look

Adult summer ▲
Big, heavy, pale grey and
white; shaggy black cap;
long black legs

▲ Bill
Big, deep red,
with marked
angle below

SUB-ADULT

WINTER

Juvenile ▶
Tail and rump mottled,
greyish, with darker
band at tip

Sandwich Tern
Sterna sandvicensis

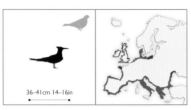

36–41cm 14–16in

DISTRIBUTION
Very local breeder on beaches, dunes; widespread migrant offshore, also on lagoons, rare inland

Flight ►
Very pale; long, narrow wings streaked darker near tip; long head and bill, short tail give mid-winged effect; white rump and tail

ADULTS

▲ From below
A very white-looking tern, with slightly darker wingtips; black bill

JUVENILE

Juvenile ▲
Darker wingtips, barred inner wing, dark corners to tail

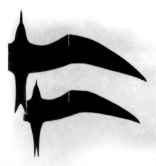

◄ Wing shapes
Sandwich tern (top) has long, narrow wings, with inner wing proportionately longer than on common tern (bottom)

IDENTIFICATION A large, long-winged tern, very pale silvery-grey and white, looking much whiter than common tern when seen in flight at a distance. Close views reveal black bill, with small yellowish tip, and black legs (never any red on bill or legs). Wingtip becomes darker in the autumn, streaked blackish. Juvenile greyer, with bars and mottling above, and dark tips to the tail feathers. Calls loud, grating, rhythmic *kee-er-rink* or *kerr-ik*. Gull-billed tern has slightly stouter body, shorter bill with no pale tip, smooth crown without crest, narrow dark trailing edge to outer wing, and a pale grey rump (which is often hard to see).

HABITAT Sand and shingle beaches, dunes, and low islands; on lagoons near the sea; also over the sea, rarely inland over lakes.

BEHAVIOUR A noisy, active, highly strung, and very social tern, breeding in dense colonies, which are easily deserted if disturbed. Feeds over the sea, diving in from a considerable height with a loud splash. Tends to fly higher over the sea than smaller terns, often far offshore.

SUMMER

◄ Spring adult
Crested black cap complete until June, then forehead becomes white (left)

JUVENILE

JUVENILE

GULL-BILLED

ADULT

Head and bill comparisons ▲
Juvenile has shorter bill than adult; juvenile gull-billed lacks paler tip, has dark eye patch

Roseate Tern
Sterna dougallii

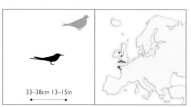

33–38cm 13–15in

DISTRIBUTION
Extremely local
breeder on Irish
Sea and North Sea
coasts; rare migrant
on shores of
W Europe

IDENTIFICATION   One of a difficult trio with common and Arctic terns, but distinctive with experience. In flight looks more like little tern, with rather quick, shallow beats of narrow, slightly blunter, shorter wings. Extremely pale, silvery above and whiter below than common or Arctic tern, recalling larger Sandwich tern, although its plumage is quite strongly tinged pink in spring. Bill black with red at base in spring; red becomes much more extensive by early autumn. Outer wing has narrow whitish trailing edge, without the dark trailing edge of the other two; paler area behind the bend of the wing from beneath is more like that of common tern than the extensively translucent wing of Arctic tern. Juvenile has much darker forehead and darker legs than the other two. Calls include distinctive bright *chi-vik* and raucous *kraak*.

HABITAT   Breeds in much reduced numbers at a handful of colonies, on rocky islands and coastal lagoons. Migrants rare over the sea or resting on beaches, and extremely rare inland.

BEHAVIOUR   Breeds in colonies, choosing sheltered nest sites, often close to other terns and gulls. Flies over the sea, hovering briefly, then diving for fish, or flying down at an angle into the water.

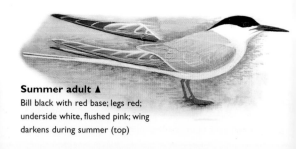

Summer adult ▲
Bill black with red base; legs red;
underside white, flushed pink; wing
darkens during summer (top)

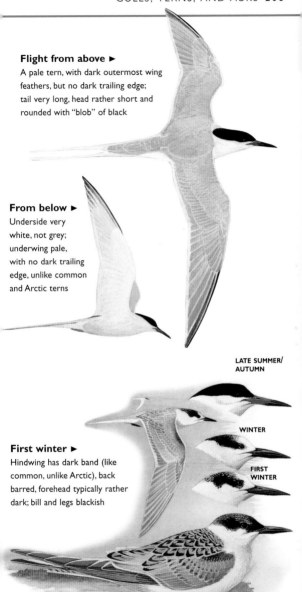

Flight from above ▶
A pale tern, with dark outermost wing feathers, but no dark trailing edge; tail very long, head rather short and rounded with "blob" of black

From below ▶
Underside very white, not grey; underwing pale, with no dark trailing edge, unlike common and Arctic terns

LATE SUMMER/ AUTUMN

WINTER

FIRST WINTER

First winter ▶
Hindwing has dark band (like common, unlike Arctic), back barred, forehead typically rather dark; bill and legs blackish

Juvenile ▶
Whole upper half of head dark at first, forehead becomes whiter; legs dark grey; buff tips on back wear off

Common Tern
Sterna hirundo

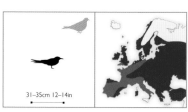

31–35cm 12–14in

DISTRIBUTION
Widespread
breeder, on coasts
and inland on
rivers, flooded
gravel pits; occurs
on most coasts

IDENTIFICATION Very like Arctic and roseate terns, but distinguishable with practice. Has slightly broader wings, longer and flatter head and neck, and shorter tail, giving longer-headed, fractionally heavier, more front-heavy look in flight than Arctic tern. Greyer than roseate, but paler beneath than Arctic tern, with less contrasting white underwings. Its legs are longer than those of Arctic tern; its bill a more vermilion-red, less deep, with a black tip. In flight, adults have a small wedge of dark grey on the hindwing towards the tip in spring; as the outer feathers wear, they become

From below ▼
Juvenile and adult have opaque
underwing and paler patch
behind angle; broad
dark trailing edge
(thin on Arctic)

▲ Juvenile
Upperside coarsely barred, washed
buff at first; darker bar along trailing
edge of inner wing, midwing paler

Adult from above ▲
Outer primaries slightly darker
than inner ones, contrast
greatest in autumn

blacker, giving a darker wingtip by autumn (on Arctic, the isolated wedge is absent and the whole upperwing looks paler and more uniform). From below, the underwing looks opaque with just a paler patch behind the angle (much more translucent throughout on Arctic). Juveniles are easy as common has a dark hindwing band and pale grey rump, while Arctic has a white hindwing and white rump. Calls include sharp *kit*, *kit-it-it-it*, *kieri kieri kieri,* and *pee-airr* with emphasis on higher first syllable (Arctic has rising call).

HABITAT Breeds on sand and shingle, on beaches, rivers, and inland waters. Widespread on coasts of all kinds, spring to autumn.

BEHAVIOUR Breeds in colonies; aggressive towards intruders and noisy. Feeds by hovering, then diving in for fish. Less hesitant than Arctic tern, which tends to dive with one or two pauses.

▼ One year old
Year-old birds usually remain in Africa and are rare in Europe; variable dark bill and legs, dark wings

Winter ▼
Rarely seen in Europe; bill and legs blackish, dark bar on forewing

FIRST SUMMER

FIRST WINTER

WINTER ADULT

SUMMER ADULT

JUVENILE

Juvenile ▶
Barred above; bill buff-red at base with dark tip; legs orange-brown to reddish; neat black cap, white forehead (buffish at first)

Arctic Tern
Sterna paradisaea

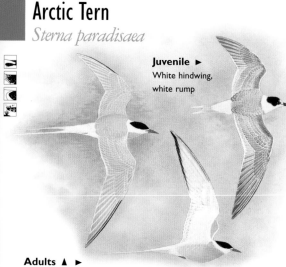

Juvenile ►
White hindwing,
white rump

Adults ▲ ►
Short bill/head/neck, long tail; narrow wings all
pale grey, even whiter towards narrow, tapered
tips; underwing white with fine dark line
towards tip, all flight feathers semi-translucent

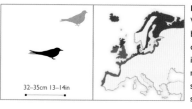

32–35cm 13–14in

DISTRIBUTION
Widespread
breeder in north,
on tundra and
islands; when on
migration widely
seen on coasts,
scarcer inland

IDENTIFICATION Compare with similar common tern: has
shorter bill, all red in summer; shorter red legs which are obvious
when perched; rounder head. In flight looks almost neckless; shorter
bill and head, and longer tail, give less mid-winged effect. Wings
taper to narrower, sharper point; very white underwing with thinner,
sharper dark line on trailing edge below and more translucent effect
against light. Upperwing paler grey, without contrast on outer wing
(combination of upper and underwing, sharp wingtip, neckless look,
and light, airy action allow identification at long range in flight).
Juvenile has whiter rump, whiter forehead, darker red base or wholly
blacker bill, whiter hindwing (obvious in flight). Calls much like

◄ First summer
Rare in Europe; common (left) more
contrasted and patchy than Arctic
on upperwing

▼ On ground
Rounded head; thick, spike-like deep
red bill; tiny red legs; grey
underside, white cheeks
and throat

FIRST SUMMER

Adult ►
Typical greyer individual; note
wingtip all pale, even when closed
(common has darker outer feathers)

AUTUMN
JUVENILE

YOUNG JUVENILE

common tern: irritable, harsh, with clearer, more piping notes, and a
rising *kree-eh* (common tern emphasizes first note; second note falls).

HABITAT Breeds on tundra and on coasts, mainly on shingle or
rocky islets. Widespread at sea and inshore on migration; occasional
flocks inland, especially in spring.

BEHAVIOUR A colonial breeder, bold and aggressive towards
intruders, even striking people who venture too close. Feeds by
flying over water, hovering and diving for fish, tending to have a
pause or "catch" in the dive before the final plunge.

Black Tern
Chlidonias niger

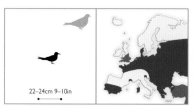

22–24cm 9–10in

DISTRIBUTION
Local breeder on
marshes, lakes;
widespread on
migration over sea,
coasts and on
inland waters

▼ Three marsh terns
Black (centre), smaller white-winged black (left)
and larger whiskered (right) are often called
"marsh terns"

WHITE-WINGED BLACK TERN   JUVENILE BLACK   WHISKERED

IDENTIFICATION One of a trio of "marsh terns" that breed on
freshwater (but migrate over the sea) and feed by dipping to the
surface rather than diving in for fish. A small, neat, black-billed tern;
in spring blackish with white under the tail, dusky underwings,
black legs and bill; in autumn grey above, white below, with a
distinctive dark mark at side of breast. Juvenile white-winged black
terns have darker backs, paler wings, and whiter rumps.

HABITAT Breeds on floods, shallow lakes, and marshes with
plentiful aquatic vegetation. Migrants at reservoirs, lakes, sea coasts.

BEHAVIOUR Feeding birds beat steadily into the wind, low over
water, sideslipping, twisting, and dipping to pick food from the
surface, then wheeling round and gliding downwind before turning
for another "run": much more like little gulls than most other terns.
Large flocks sometimes appear over reservoirs, staying for a day or
two, or moving on very quickly.

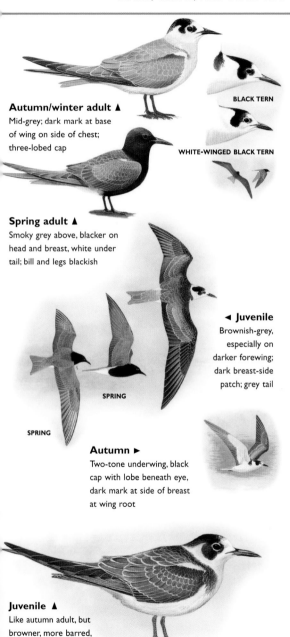

Autumn/winter adult ▲
Mid-grey; dark mark at base
of wing on side of chest;
three-lobed cap

BLACK TERN

WHITE-WINGED BLACK TERN

Spring adult ▲
Smoky grey above, blacker on
head and breast, white under
tail; bill and legs blackish

◄ Juvenile
Brownish-grey,
especially on
darker forewing;
dark breast-side
patch; grey tail

SPRING

SPRING

Autumn ►
Two-tone underwing, black
cap with lobe beneath eye,
dark mark at side of breast
at wing root

Juvenile ▲
Like autumn adult, but
browner, more barred,
with pale feather tips

White-winged Black Tern
Chlidonias leucopterus

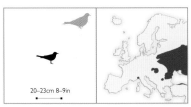

20–23cm 8–9in

DISTRIBUTION
Very local breeder
on wet marshes,
lakes in E Europe;
rare but regular
migrant in west,
often inland

Winter adult ▼
Pale; no breast marking (see
black tern); short black bill,
longish red legs

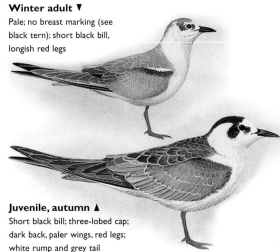

Juvenile, autumn ▲
Short black bill; three-lobed cap;
dark back, paler wings, red legs;
white rump and grey tail

IDENTIFICATION A small marsh tern, rather like black tern,
but deeper-bodied, longer-legged, and shorter-billed. Summer adult
has eyecatching pattern, with white upperwing, rump, and tail quite
unlike black tern or whiskered tern. Winter adult more difficult, but
white breast with no dark side patches and white rump distinctive.
Autumn juvenile (typical migrant in W Europe) has dark saddle, all-
white breast, and white rump. Flight less dainty than black tern.

HABITAT Breeds in extensive marshes with rivers, floods, lakes;
migrants over coastal pools, lakes, and reservoirs.

BEHAVIOUR Much the same as black tern and whiskered tern;
usually seen perched on a post or buoy, or flying low over water, but
with a straighter, steadier flight. Often found singly, mixed with
larger numbers of black terns.

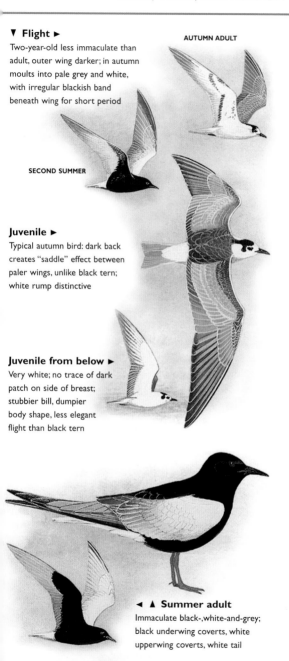

▼ Flight ►

Two-year-old less immaculate than adult, outer wing darker; in autumn moults into pale grey and white, with irregular blackish band beneath wing for short period

AUTUMN ADULT

SECOND SUMMER

Juvenile ►

Typical autumn bird: dark back creates "saddle" effect between paler wings, unlike black tern; white rump distinctive

Juvenile from below ►

Very white; no trace of dark patch on side of breast; stubbier bill, dumpier body shape, less elegant flight than black tern

◄ ▲ Summer adult

Immaculate black-,white-and-grey; black underwing coverts, white upperwing coverts, white tail

Whiskered Tern
Chlidonias hybridus

24–28cm 9–11in

DISTRIBUTION
Local breeding bird on marshes and reed-fringed rivers; rare outside usual breeding range in spring and autumn

IDENTIFICATION The largest "marsh tern", easily identified in summer by the combination of a pale grey rump, pale upperside, black cap, white face and underwing, and blackish underside. Dark red bill is longer and thicker than on black or white-winged black terns. In winter it is more like white-winged black, but has a longer bill, black streaks on the crown with a more discrete black eyepatch, and a grey rump. Autumn juveniles tricky: greyish with some dark bars above, greyer rump than white-winged black, paler wings than black tern, longer bill and legs. Winter birds are more like common terns, but shorter, squarer, greyer tail and a different head pattern help identify them.

HABITAT Reed-fringed rivers and lakes, river deltas and fringes of estuaries, rice paddies and other flooded areas, coastal lagoons.

BEHAVIOUR Much like black and white-winged black terns, flying low over water and marshy places, dipping to the surface to find food, sometimes diving down from a greater height, but barely entering the water. Breeds in small, loose colonies.

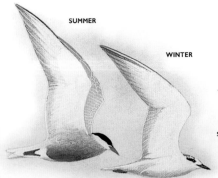

SUMMER

WINTER

◄ Adults
White underwing; dark belly, white face, black cap in summer; black eye patch, streaked crown in winter

Winter adult ►
Three-lobed black cap blurs
onto streaked crown, larger
than on white-winged black;
grey rump and tail; pale wings

▲ Summer adult
Pale grey upperside, including
rump and tail; black cap; red bill

Summer adult ▼
Black cap; white cheeks and
throat create white-faced effect
against dark grey-black underside;
deep red bill, red legs

Juvenile ►
Coarsely barred back soon
becomes pale grey; thick, long,
black bill; longish red legs

Guillemot
Uria aalge

38–45cm 15–18in

DISTRIBUTION
Localized breeder on sheer sea cliffs, offshore stacks; widespread inshore, but mostly far out at sea in winter

Flight ▼
Brown (southern) or blackish above, short tail, spike-like beak, heavy body; white sides to dark rump

Flight ▼
Typical bird dark with white belly and underwing; northern form has barred underwing and dark throat band

NORTHERN FORM

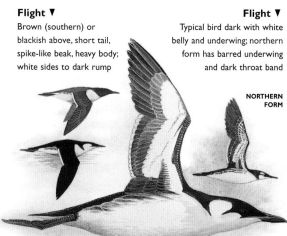

IDENTIFICATION Heavy-bodied, narrow-winged seabird with short legs, unable to walk, but stands on narrow cliff ledges. Flies fast, low, and direct over sea, swims buoyantly. In W Europe browner than razorbill, but in north almost as black. Bill dagger-like with no white lines, tail square. In winter has white line on hindwing when swimming (unlike, for example, grebes or much larger divers); note bill shape and head pattern. Loud whirring and growling calls at colony; juvenile at sea makes far-carrying, whistling trill.

HABITAT Open sea in winter; inshore waters, larger bays and firths in summer, nesting on sheer cliffs and offshore stacks.

BEHAVIOUR Breeds in dense, noisy colonies, often with razorbills and kittiwakes. Large numbers swim on sea below breeding cliffs, or fly in and out of the busy colony. Dives underwater for fish.

◄ Summer
Dark brown and white
(northern birds blacker),
with sharp, pointed bill
and short, square tail

Head patterns ▼
By August (left) loses dark
throat; in winter (right)
has white face with short
dark line behind eye

"Bridled" form ►
Small number have white
eye-ring and line behind
eye; increasingly common
farther north, interbreed
with normal form

Winter ▼
Looks long but quite squat on water, with
head hunched down, tail slightly raised;
big white cheek patch with dark line

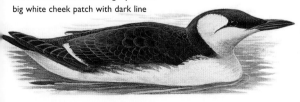

Black Guillemot
Cepphus grylle

30–32cm 12–14in

DISTRIBUTION
Local breeder on rocky shores, islets; does not move far in winter, scarce on coasts of NW Europe

▼ **Flight patterns**
Bold white patch above and below wing; otherwise all dark in summer; paler, barred dark in winter

SUMMER

WINTER

▼ **Immature stages**
Juvenile dark with white bars on wing patch; first winter paler on head and neck

JUVENILE

FIRST WINTER

IDENTIFICATION Simple in summer, being a small, dark, buoyant seabird with a large white patch each side of the black body. In flight, or when flapping its wings, patch revealed as a white oval on the upperwing, plus a big white patch on the underwing. More confusing in winter and immature plumages, with mottled, less eyecatching black, white, and grey patterns, more like small grebe or strange duck, but small size, clear white wing patch of adult, barred patch on immature, whitish head and neck, and barred back all help, together with pointed tail (ruling out grebes) and short, sharp bill. In summer makes shrill whistles and rapid, high-pitched trills.

HABITAT Does not join large seabird colonies on cliffs, but nests in holes on islets, rocky beaches, and scree slopes, typically around islands in quite wide bays and firths, or in channels between island groups. Spends the winter in sheltered inshore waters.

BEHAVIOUR Tends to swim just offshore in ones, twos, or family groups, diving frequently when feeding or bobbing like a cork on the waves. Also rests on low rocks, when red legs are easily visible. Sometimes blown inshore, south of usual range, by winter storms.

Summer ►
Smoky black with white wing patch, red legs, red inside mouth

▲ On sea
Small, dumpy, dagger bill; often rises up to flap wings, revealing white patches

FIRST SUMMER

WINTER ADULT

◄ Winter
Like small grebe with clear white wing patch, pointed tail

Little Auk
Alle alle

17–19cm 7in

DISTRIBUTION
Arctic breeder; scarce in northern seas in winter, rare but regular in variable numbers in North Sea

WINTER

▲ Flight
Small, dumpy, with narrow wings; groups fly low, fast, almost like small waders

Summer ►
Black and white, stubby bill, lacy white lines on shoulders

WINTER

▼ Winter
Dark cap to below eye, white crescent on neck; head up when alert and fit, hunched down when exhausted

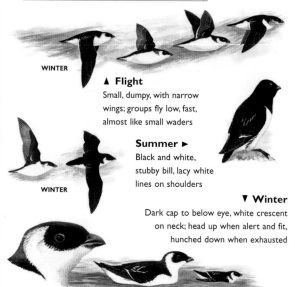

IDENTIFICATION A small, rounded, frog-headed seabird with a short, black bill. In summer whole head and bib black; in winter face and throat white, with black cap. Short bill and pointed tail rule out small grebes. Often dives with wings slightly open. Fast flight, often rolling sideways, with quick, flickering wingbeats; underwing looks dark. Smaller than puffin, with smaller, blacker bill.

HABITAT Breeds on cliffs and screes of Arctic coasts and islands. In winter at sea, sometimes blown inshore (rarely inland) by gales.

BEHAVIOUR In western Europe, usually seen flying by headlands in late autumn, especially in strong onshore winds, but exhausted birds may remain on coastal pools or in harbours and bays for a time.

Razorbill
Alca torda

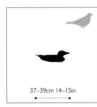
37–39cm 14–15in

DISTRIBUTION
Local nester on sea cliffs; in autumn in some estuaries, but mostly well out at sea outside breeding season

▼ **Bill details**
Bill smaller in winter, face dark; in summer has larger bill crossed by white line, and white line from bill to eye

SUMMER

▼ **Adult**
Black face and throat in summer; white in winter, black cap reaches beneath eye

WINTER

JUVENILE

WINTER

On water ▲
Pointed tail often raised; thicker bill, larger head than guillemot

WINTER

IDENTIFICATION A rather large, heavy-bodied, big-headed auk, with a longer, more pointed tail and blunter bill than guillemot. Thick bill visible at reasonable range; in summer white stripe to eye is diagnostic. In winter black cap reaches below eye level; no dark stripe on white cheek as on guillemot. In flight looks blacker above than southern guillemots, but this distinction less useful northwards from Scotland, as guillemots become black-backed.

HABITAT Breeds in cavities and on sheltered ledges on sea cliffs, on less open sites than guillemot. Otherwise mostly out at sea, but may feed close inshore or at estuary mouths in summer and autumn.

BEHAVIOUR Social breeder, usually less abundant than guillemot in mixed colonies. Large numbers often on sea below colony.

Puffin

Fratercula arctica

Adults ▼
Black and white, bright bill; face
and smaller bill darker in winter;
orange legs distinctive

WINTER

BREEDING

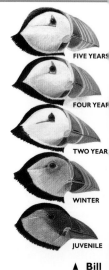

FIVE YEARS

FOUR YEARS

TWO YEARS

WINTER

JUVENILE

▲ Bill
Bright summer bill develops
with age (top three); reduced
in winter, smallest in juvenile

26–29cm 10–11in

DISTRIBUTION
Local nester on
islands and rocky
coasts; scarce
migrant offshore,
otherwise well out
at sea in winter

IDENTIFICATION A small, dumpy, black-and-white seabird,
with a large, colourful bill and orange legs. In summer has disc-like
greyish face patch, dark crown and breastband. In winter, face darker
grey, bill smaller, darker; juvenile has even smaller bill and lacks
bright colours. Flight fast and whirring, usually low and direct, head
and bill looking thicker than little auk. On water looks small, with
short, square tail slightly raised, head hunched down.

HABITAT Breeds in burrows on grassy slopes above cliffs, scree
slopes; on more indented cliffs, not on open ledges. At sea in winter.

BEHAVIOUR More agile on land than other auks, walking around
burrows, looking merely curious, but often aggressive to other
puffins. Often sits outside burrow, or stands on cliff ledge near deep
cavity, before flying off fast and diving down to the sea.

Rock Dove
Columba livia

31–35cm 12–14in

DISTRIBUTION
Truly wild birds local in north; domestic pigeons gone wild very widespread, from towns to cliffs

IDENTIFICATION Feral ("gone wild") pigeons can be many colours, often blackish or smoky grey, but many look much like their wild ancestor the rock dove, which is handsome grey, paler above, with double dark bars on wing and white rump. White underwing unlike stock dove. Wild birds have tiny white, fleshy knob at base of bill (cere); this is usually much bigger on domestic descendants.

HABITAT True rock doves breed on cliffs, but feed on adjacent grassy areas and cultivated fields. Feral birds occupy similar habitats, but also extend to quarries, towns, and city buildings, and feed more widely on all kinds of agricultural land and urban/suburban areas.

BEHAVIOUR Much like familiar town pigeon; very fast and agile in flight around sea cliffs, dashing into deep caves.

▼ Flight
Two black wingbars, white rump; small head and bill

Head and bill ▶
Wild rock dove has fine bill; town pigeon (lower) is thick-billed

Kingfisher
Alcedo atthis

16–17cm 7in

DISTRIBUTION
Widespread
breeder; in winter
moves to coasts,
including estuary
creeks, especially in
severe weather

Flight ▶
Fast and direct; looks front-
heavy; may show colours or just
streak of blue on middle of back

MALE

FEMALE

▼ Perched
Big head and dagger bill give
unique silhouette; white
patches help camouflage
among overhanging
leaves or against
rippling water

Nest ▶
Nests in long
tunnel in bank
over water

IDENTIFICATION Starling-sized, rather elusive despite bright
colours, often detected by first hearing sharp, high *chi-keee* call. In
flight shows electric-blue back, blue-green wings, orange underside,
very short trail, but large head and bill. Perched, may look bluish or
greener, depending on light, with striking white cheek patch and
rusty-orange chest. Dagger bill orange at base on female.
HABITAT Creeks, streams, ditches, edges of lakes and rivers.
BEHAVIOUR Sits patiently above water's edge waiting for fish,
caught in dive with loud "plop". Flies low and direct over water.

Shore Lark
Eremophila alpestris

DISTRIBUTION
Scarce and local breeder in north; equally local in winter on low-lying coasts with sand, muddy marshes

14–17cm 6–7in

▼ Winter
Quite plain body and wings, tail edged white; black-and-yellow face pattern diagnostic

MALE

FEMALES

FEMALE

TAIL

MALE

▲ Variation
Rare breeders in Balkans (top) grey above; female (lower) lacks "horns"

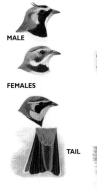

IDENTIFICATION Skylark-sized but slimmer, a neat, low-slung, long-tailed lark with striking head pattern and black legs (pale on skylark). Winter males show black and yellow on face, black and brown breastband; yellow brighter in spring, black more extensive. Females and young birds duller, but show trace of pattern, with black crescent below eye, black bib, faint yellow on face. Tail has pale centre, white sides. Calls thin, pipit-like *tseep* or *tseee*.

HABITAT In winter usually on edges of saltmarsh, in muddy areas behind dunes with washed-up plant debris, on tideline, or sometimes out on open, wet sandy beaches. Occasionally on grassy or ploughed fields just inland.

BEHAVIOUR Usually in small flocks or groups; inconspicuous, feeding quietly or running on the ground.

Lesser Short-toed Lark
Calandrella rufescens

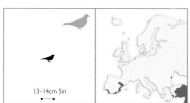

13–14cm 5in

DISTRIBUTION
Very local in Iberia, often on coasts and on dried-up mud beside rivers; very rarely outside normal range

▼ **Female**
Slightly shorter wingtip projection (dark primary feathers beyond sandy-brown tertials) than male, but longer than short-toed lark

Male ▼
Small, streaky, brown lark, with white underside, gorget of fine streaks on breast

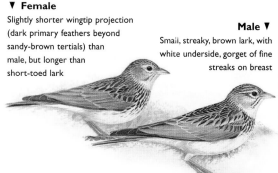

IDENTIFICATION A small, neat, brown lark, very like commoner short-toed lark, but distinguishable with experience and a good view. Looks like a miniature skylark, with a rounder head and shorter crest (sometimes raised in blunt tuft), and a short, stubby bill. Crown finely streaked; breast pale with neat, close, dark streaking overall (short-toed has more rufous crest, and pale buff or whitish breast with dark marks only at sides). Wingtips project a little beyond the long, pale-edged tertials when closed (hardly visible on short-toed). Characteristic calls include a soft, buzzy, churring *drrrr*, often included in rich, trilling, musical song with frequent mimicry (short-toed phrases shorter, less throaty, with "spitting" quality).

HABITAT Typical of drier, sandy areas with low scrub and grass at upper edge of saltmarsh, or in extensive salty coastal scrub. Also on areas of open mud that dry out in spring and summer.

BEHAVIOUR Often in small flocks, sometimes mixed with, or close to, short-toed larks. Feeds quietly on ground, hidden in low vegetation and easily overlooked until flushed.

◄ Female
Slightly shorter tail than male,
but same pattern

◄ Male in flight
Wings plainer than short-toed
lark (which has two paler wing
bars); no pale trailing edge
(unlike skylark); white-edged
tail (unlike crested lark)

▼ Variation
Spanish birds (upper) have thin bill;
those from Middle East and North
Africa (lower) have thicker, finch-like
bill; short crest can be raised

▼ Turkish race
Birds from Turkey more like
short-toed, with finer breast
streaks (absent or very faint
on short-toed)

TAIL

Crested Lark
Galerida cristata

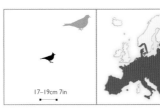

17–19cm 7in

DISTRIBUTION
Widespread, especially in S Europe, on coasts and inland; very rare outside regular nesting range

◄ Flight from below
Underwing largely orange-buff, often easy to see (thekla lark greyer, often much harder to confirm)

◄ Flight from above
Plain upperside, greyish to sandy-brown, rump similar to back (thekla has rufous area above tail); tail edged orange-buff

IDENTIFICATION A medium-large lark, looking shorter-tailed, broader-winged, and often paler than skylark, but rather variable in colour. Often tends to look pale sandy-buff, but can be greyer or browner, with dark tail edged more rusty-brown. Underwing pale, flushed with rusty-orange. Very similar thekla lark unlikely on most shores, usually browner/greyer, with heavier breast streaking, rusty patch above tail, greyer underwings (hard to see). Skylark has shorter, blunter crest, white trailing edge to wings and white tail sides. Calls rich, fluty, plaintive *tree-leee-peuw*; song includes notes of similar quality and musical whistles, in high, circling song flight.

HABITAT Open ground of all kinds, from fields to dunes, upper edge of sandy beaches and marshes, embankments around salinas and coastal lagoons; sometimes waste ground in urban areas.

BEHAVIOUR Feeds inconspicuously on ground, but often flies up and calls; or sits on stone, stump, or roof calling loudly.

Variable shapes ►
Looks round and hunched in cold weather, or thin and elongated when feathers sleeked down in hot weather

On ground ▼
Streaky brown; crest longer, more pointed than skylark's, projecting when flattened, spike-like when raised

TAIL

◄ Bill shape
Varies, usually more curved than thekla's

Meadow Pipit
Anthus pratensis

14–15cm 6in

DISTRIBUTION
Common and widespread breeder, numerous coastal migrant and winter visitor to marshes and coastal fields

IDENTIFICATION A small, slender pipit: a bird with a wagtail-like build but lark-like colouring. Walks and runs on open ground or in short grass. Other pipits confusingly similar, but meadow pipit has pale orange-pink legs; grey-brown, olive, or sandy-brown back with dark streaks; white tail sides; pale cream to buff underside with black streaks extending well down onto flanks; rather weak head pattern with short pale line over eye, and pale eye-ring. Looks weak and hesitant in short flights, more direct over long distances. Frequent sharp, peevish, nervous calls, such as *seeep*, *seee-eep*, and firmer *pip* and *pip-it*. Song is a long series of thin, sharp notes given in rising flight followed by "parachuting" descent on half-open wings.

HABITAT Breeds on moors, heaths, tundra, grassy places. At other times on all kinds of lower, open ground, including grass and ploughed fields, saltmarshes, beaches, edges of lagoons.

BEHAVIOUR Although a rather nervous bird, with distinctive "worried" calls, it is often quite approachable and easy to see. Typically feeds on the ground, but may perch in trees, especially near the nest. In winter occurs in flocks, sometimes of scores or hundreds, or in small groups. In spring and autumn small groups of migrants can be found all along freshwater and sea shores, or flying overhead.

◄ Perched
Streaked upperside, dark tail with white sides, pale underside with streaked sides all confirm "pipit"

▼ Flock in flight
Makes loose flock, moving in same general direction, but not coordinated or tightly packed

Flight ►
Small, hesitant, slightly bounding, with broad wings and longish, slim tail (shorter than any wagtail's) with white tail sides

TAIL

Comparison with tree pipit ▼
Tree pipit (top) is sleeker, with shorter hind claw, stronger head pattern; streaks peter out on buffer flanks, stronger whitish wingbar

TREE PIPIT

▼ Head pattern
Fine bill, round head, faint pale eye-ring; slight pale stripe over eye; pale stripe below cheek, dark moustache

ROCK PIPIT

SONG FLIGHT

Autumn ►
Juveniles can be more olive (above) or yellowish (below); typical long hind claw helpful

Rock Pipit
Anthus petrosus

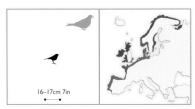

16–17cm 7in

DISTRIBUTION
Common breeding
bird on northern
coasts; scarce
migrant inland and
on low-lying coasts
in winter

IDENTIFICATION   The rock pipit of Britain, Ireland, and northern France is a larger, greyer bird than the meadow pipit, with a more blurred underside, less streaked back, grey outer tail feathers, and dark legs. Scandinavian rock pipits are similar in winter, but have greyer heads, a whiter stripe over the eye, reduced streaking below, and a pinkish-buff flush to the breast in spring. Call is fuller, lower, more forceful than meadow pipit, *fist* or *feest*. Song like meadow pipit, but louder, more trilling, in similar song flight.

Breeding ►
Darker above, whiter below
than in autumn and
winter

AUTUMN

JUVENILE

**WESTERN
SCOTLAND**

◄ Variation
Varies a little with age,
season and location;
Scandinavian birds more
like water pipit

HABITAT Rocky shores and cliffs; also muddy creeks in winter.
BEHAVIOUR Feeds on grassy areas above cliffs in summer, but more on the shore at other times, in beds of seaweed, on strandlines and on shingle beaches. Also on saltmarshes, along promenades, and on the structures of piers and jetties in winter. Tends to fly a short distance along the shore if disturbed; less wary than water pipit.

Adult ►
Quite dull pipit with drab grey-olive upperparts, yellow-buff underparts with blurred grey streaks; dark legs; often has upright stance

◄ Flight impression
Stronger, more direct than meadow pipit; darker above; sides of tail smoky-grey, not pure white

Water Pipit
Anthus spinoletta

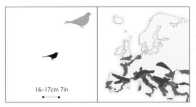

16–17cm 7in

DISTRIBUTION
Breeds on high mountain pastures; in winter moves north, west, and downhill to muddy shores, marshes

Spring ▼
Thickset pipit, recalling wheatear, with grey head, white stripe over eye, pale wingbars, pink to buff underside, dark legs

▼ Late summer
Fades paler, greyer, whiter below, with little streaking; whitish wingbars still evident

LATE SUMMER

BREEDING

ROCK   SCANDINAVIAN ROCK   WATER

IDENTIFICATION Simple in summer: a grey-headed, pink-breasted pipit with dark legs, found on very high ground. In winter occurs on low shores and muddy lagoons; more like rock but whiter below, whiter wingbars, white outer tail feathers. Scandinavian rock similar, but less pink below; more streaked in summer, weaker stripe over eye in winter (sometime seen on coasts and inland in UK).

HABITAT Breeds on open, grassy, and rocky places high in the Alps and Pyrenees, but winters on low-lying coasts, coastal marshes and pools, and around muddy lakes and floods inland.

BEHAVIOUR Much like meadow pipit in summer, feeding in open, grassy places, but also perching freely on rocks; has similar high, then parachuting, song flight. In winter it is usually wary and quick to fly off when approached, often going high and far away, almost out of sight, before settling again.

▼ **Winter**
Greyish above; long white stripe over eye; white bib outlined by dark moustaches and streaks on chest; two white wingbars

▼ **Scandinavian rock**
Much like water pipit, but browner; darker moustachial stripe in spring, often less pinkish below

SCANDINAVIAN
ROCK PIPIT

WINTER

JUVENILE

Redstart
Phoenicurus phoenicurus

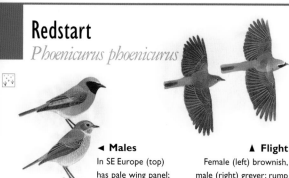

◄ Males
In SE Europe (top) has pale wing panel; duller in autumn

▲ Flight
Female (left) brownish, male (right) greyer; rump and tail sides rusty orange

DISTRIBUTION
Widespread breeding bird in woodland; common migrant on many coasts, in scrub, trees, dunes

13–14cm 5in

IDENTIFICATION Spring males are easy to tell, with pale grey upperside, white forehead, black face, and orange breast. Females and autumn birds paler, buff-brown with pale grey-brown back, variable pale orange-buff below; note dark eye in plain face. Orange-red rump and tail (often flickered) obvious, especially in flight. Autumn males have bright face and body colours obscured by pale edges to feathers, but tail remains striking. Looks rather like a slender robin in size and shape. Calls include sweet *hweet* followed by hard tapping notes, *hweet tac tac* or *hweet-tik*.

HABITAT Spring and autumn migrants in coastal woods, isolated trees, thickets, and bushes; sometimes in low vegetation on dunes.

BEHAVIOUR Migrants are often quite secretive, but generally reveal themselves by flying down to the ground to pick up food and back up to a perch again, or flitting out to catch a fly in mid-air. They often flick or vibrate their bright tails.

◄ Variation
Spring male (left) has bold black face, white forehead; female (middle) and juvenile (right) duller, plainer

Black Redstart
Phoenicurus ochruros

13–14cm 5in

DISTRIBUTION
Breeds in urban areas, and on cliffs in mountain regions; in autumn and winter occurs on low-lying coasts

◄ First winter
Male (top) and female (lower) both quite pale smoky-grey, more or less tinged brown; plain face except for pale eye-ring; rusty tail

▼ Flight
Darker, greyer than redstart, rusty tail, bright rump less extensive

Variation ▲
Iberian males (top) blackest; other males (centre) dark with whitish wing panel; females (lower) greyer

IDENTIFICATION A small, greyish, robin-like chat; always less buff or brown than female redstart, greyer overall, with rufous patch above tail more restricted to upper tail coverts, less on rump. Males black on face, with paler grey cap, and white wing panel (but can breed in greyer immature plumage). Females and young birds grey below, not buff, tinged brown in winter. Calls include scratchy notes and sharp, whistled *pi-sit*, but a quiet bird in autumn and winter.

HABITAT Breeds in towns, industrial sites, waste ground, and cliffs inland. Migrants move to lower ground in autumn and winter; often in quarries, along stony shores and bays, and on waste ground with ruins, boulders, or small buildings along coastal strip.

BEHAVIOUR Perches high on cliffs or on buildings, but migrants usually keep on or near the ground. Rather inconspicuous.

Stonechat

Saxicola torquata

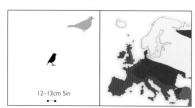

12–13cm 5in

DISTRIBUTION
Widespread but local on heaths, moors; in winter many move to coastal heaths, waste ground

IDENTIFICATION A small, rounded chat, rather like a short-tailed robin, much smaller than wheatear, typically seen perched on top of a bush or tall stem, or on an overhead wire, not usually inside thick vegetation. Male distinctive with black face and throat, reddish chest, black tail; in autumn and winter much less contrasty, with rich orange-brown colours, but still at least a hint of white neck patch and dark chin. Female usually paler, with brown throat (streaked and outlined with buff in winter) and pale line over the eye (similar whinchat has white each side of tail, paler chin, and is only a spring to autumn visitor to Europe). Calls include hard tacking notes and bright whistle, often combined as *see tak tak*.

HABITAT Heaths and rough ground of many kinds, especially with tall heather and gorse, but in winter also unkempt grassy places with tall stems and scattered bushes, often with stones or boulders.

BEHAVIOUR Often approachable, but calls in alarm when people are near, or scolds noisily when nesting, usually from an exposed perch. Looks for food on the ground while perched, then drops down to pick it up, like a miniature (but far less predatory) shrike. In winter, often two or three together, but usually keeping a few metres apart, maintaining contact with frequent calls.

◄ Autumn male
Brightness of summer obscured by paler feather tips, giving browner look overall

Flying away ▼

A small, flitting, dark bird, with all-dark tail, but white patches on inner wing (whinchat has white triangle each side of tail)

Flight ▼

Male has striking white patches on shoulders, variable whitish rump

Summer male ▶

Pale buff feather tips wear off to reveal black above and whiter underside, more contrasted than in winter

◀ Winter male

Duller, less contrasted than in summer, more extensive orange-buff below; blackish throat, white neck patch

▼ Females and immatures

Pale line over eye, dark face and throat, all-dark tail (whinchat has bolder stripe over eye, pale throat, white-sided tail)

▼ Male

Black head, white collar, rufous-orange chest, white patch on blackish wing

YOUNG FEMALE

DARK-THROATED FEMALE

YOUNG MALE

MALE

FEMALE

Wheatear
Oenanthe oenanthe

15cm 6in

DISTRIBUTION
Breeds on moors
and heaths, but
common migrant
on grassy areas,
fields, waste ground
near coasts

UNDERSIDE

Flight ▲
Striking white rump and tail with
black T-shaped tail pattern

**FEMALE AND
AUTUMN MALE**

SPRING MALE

IDENTIFICATION Larger than a robin or stonechat; a stocky, bold, terrestrial chat with an upright stance. When approached, tends to squat momentarily, then fly away fast and low, but not far, revealing big white rump and characteristic dark T-shaped tail band/centre: only rarer black-eared and pied wheatears have similar pattern. Males in spring bright and eyecatching; females easier to overlook on ground, being browner and without the black eyepatch. Calls include a hard, clicking *tsak* and a low, short whistle.

HABITAT Breeds on moors and heaths with stones, boulders, rabbit holes, and areas of short grass. Migrants like grassy places, from golf courses and fields to saltmarsh edges and dunes, close to coast.

BEHAVIOUR Characteristically a ground-loving bird, not often perching on tall or thin vegetation, but often on fence posts, walls, wires. Feeds by moving forward quickly, stopping in an upright stance, moving again, dipping forward to pick food from ground.

▼ Spring and summer

Adult male (centre) pale grey with black eye patch, blackish wings, pale underside variably tinged orange-buff to cream; female (right) duller

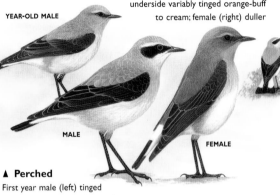

YEAR-OLD MALE

MALE

FEMALE

▲ Perched

First year male (left) tinged brownish; adult male clean and bright (Spanish birds, far right, especially so); female has browner back, less distinct face pattern

Variations ▼

Great variation with age, sex, and season; autumn birds bright buff with obscure face patterns

JUVENILE

AUTUMN MALE

▲ Autumn

Males, females, and juveniles similar, bright, buffy, with orange-buff on wing feathers, but all have distinctive rump and tail

JUVENILE "GREENLAND"

MALE "GREENLAND"

▲ Greenland breeders

Migrants from Greenland larger; back bluish-grey mixed with brown, underside of male brighter orange-buff

Jackdaw
Corvus monedula

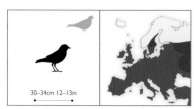

30–34cm 12–13in

DISTRIBUTION
Breeds in towns, quarries, cliffs, often along coasts; in winter on lower ground, in fields, grassland, parks

IDENTIFICATION A small, greyish crow, easily identified, but easily overlooked in groups of larger rooks. Black cap and chin contrasting with greyer neck obvious, white eye distinctive. (Hooded crow has black head and neck, but grey body.) Chief problem is distinguishing jackdaws from choughs on rocky coasts and cliffs: chough has squarer, more deeply fingered wings; more sharply square-cut tail; longer, more protruding head and bill in flight; even more acrobatic flight with typically "bouncy" or bounding action, as well as distinctive red bill and legs in close view. Jackdaw's calls include variations on short, slightly squeaky or musical *chak*, *jak*, and *chiak* notes.

HABITAT Typical of old woodland, parkland, farmland with trees, town parks, buildings, city centres, quarries, and cliffs, including high sea cliffs on many coasts.

BEHAVIOUR A social crow, often mixing with rooks, woodpigeons, and, where they occur, choughs. Frequently soars around pinnacles, or tall buildings with chimneys and towers, gliding easily, but periodically scattering or diving down in agile twisting flight, with a burst of loud, excited calls. Feeds on the ground, often on beaches, walking slowly forward and picking up food, sometimes digging into soft soil or sand.

▼ **Compare with rook**

Rook larger, longer-winged; tail longer, more rounded, head protrudes more

ROOK

ROOK

JACKDAWS

▼ Flight shapes
Quite pigeon-like, but broader wings with rounder tips, often curved back; deep body; short, blunt head and bill

Flight ▼
Often in tight flocks, soaring or diving, twisting, chasing; mixes with rooks, when smaller size is simplest clue

GLIDING

SOARING

DIRECT FLIGHT

▼ On ground
Note black cap and chin, with pale eye; pale grey neck and greyish underside, bluish-slate back, blacker wings and tail

Western Europe ▼
Handsome at close range; tinged bluish; shiny black cap, whitish eye characteristic in good view

▲ Juvenile
Duller; darker eye

▲ Northern Europe
Paler collar, whitish mark at base of side of neck, but worn plumage is duller and darker

Daurian jackdaw ▲
Rare vagrant from Siberia

Raven
Corvus corax

54–67cm 21–26in

DISTRIBUTION
Breeds on cliffs or in trees near heaths and moors, inland and on the coast; in winter roams widely in similar areas and habitats

▼ Perched

Massive black crow, with flat or peaked head; long, thick, arched bill; throat feathers sleeked flat or raised in spiky "beard"

IDENTIFICATION The largest crow; all-black, with blue and violet sheen. Often located and identified by calls, which include loud, throaty *prruk prruk*, more ringing *tok*, and deep, rolling *crronk*, all far-carrying, more powerful than carrion crow. In flight protruding head and neck usually obvious; closed or slightly fanned tail has distinct wedge-shaped tip; wings long, tapered, often angled back, but spread wide and flat when soaring. Close views reveal heavy head and long, arched bill. May fly, or perch, with feathers of crown raised and throat feathers erect, giving grotesquely large-headed effect. Juvenile similar, but wings and tail shorter at first, more like black-faced, large-billed, oversized rook.

HABITAT All kinds of open ground, from remote moors and mountains, cliffs and quarries, to woods, fields, farmland, and even urban areas, over which it often flies. Frequent on rocky coasts.

BEHAVIOUR A bold predator, capable of killing hares and rabbits, and medium-sized birds if it can catch them, but usually feeds on dead animals such as sheep and deer in the hills. Powerful in the air, circling and soaring with great skill; acrobatic flight over cliffs.

Flying away ▶
Rounded tail, pointed wings
can recall rook, but raven is
bigger, more powerful bird,
with more wedge-shaped or
diamond-shaped tail

◀ Flight
Long, flat-backed look, with big,
angular, fingered wings, often
swept back; moulting birds often
have gap behind bend of wing

▼ From below
Long head and bill; broad, wedge-
shaped tail, rounder when fanned

Flight ▲
Uniquely rolls over onto
back, then rolls back
again in flight

▲ Soaring
Soars and circles at a
height like a large, black
bird of prey

▲ Flight shapes
Cross-shaped, with fingered
wingtips and bulging trailing
edge to inner wing

◀ Raised "beard"
Loose hackles on
throat give ragged,
big-headed look

Chough
Pyrrhocorax pyrrhocorax

▼ **On ground**
Sleek, tapered, short-tailed; round head, curved red bill obvious

37–41cm 15–16in

DISTRIBUTION
Common in high mountain ranges, less so along W European coasts; rare outside breeding range

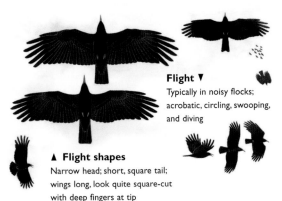

Flight ▼
Typically in noisy flocks; acrobatic, circling, swooping, and diving

▲ **Flight shapes**
Narrow head; short, square tail; wings long, look quite square-cut with deep fingers at tip

IDENTIFICATION Medium-sized crow; all glossy black except for red bill and legs (bill shorter, dull orange on juvenile). Bill slightly curved. Broad, square wings and short, square tail distinguish it from jackdaw and larger carrion crow. Calls distinctive, more squealing, ringing, or challenging than jackdaw, but some short, clipped notes: *peeeyah*, *chiaaar*, *tee-er*, *chuff*.

HABITAT Inland and coastal cliffs, quarries, mine shafts; feeds on old pastures and moors, also sandy beaches and tidelines in winter.

BEHAVIOUR Almost always in pairs or larger groups, sometimes large, tight flocks, feeding on the ground; often on cliff ledges.

Twite
Carduelis flavirostris

DISTRIBUTION
Scarce breeding
bird on moors,
meadows, often
close to coast; in
winter mostly on
saltmarshes

13–14cm 5in

IDENTIFICATION A small, linnet-like finch, without the red crown and breast or unmarked chestnut back of male linnet. Looks more like redpoll, with streaked buff-brown plumage and obvious buff wingbar, but with linnet's white streaks in wings and tail. Broad tawny-buff throat, streaked buff flanks. Male has deep pink rump. Bill distinctive yellow in winter. Calls include harder chatter than linnet, and twanging, nasal *twa-eet*.

HABITAT Breeds around hay meadows and smallholdings near coasts, mostly in upland areas, but winters near shore on saltmarshes and adjacent rough, grassy places.

BEHAVIOUR Much like commoner linnet, tending to feed and fly around marsh in similar tight-knit, bounding flocks, often "disappearing" in vegetation when settled.

◀ Perched
Scandinavian birds (top) very buff;
W European ones darker; recalls
redpoll, with buff wingbar, but white
streak on wings and
plain, buff throat

Flight ▲
Small, compact; white streaks on
wing and tail sides like linnet

Linnet
Carduelis cannabina

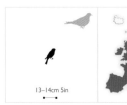

13–14cm 5in

DISTRIBUTION
Widespread in
summer on heaths,
farmland; common
coastal migrant in
spring and autumn,
fewer in winter

IDENTIFICATION A small, quite long, slender finch, with a deeply notched tail. Shows pale marks on head at all ages: a line above the eye and a pale spot on the cheek. Small, grey bill (yellow on twite in winter). Pale bar across closed wing much less evident than on twite or redpoll, but long white streaks on outer wing and white sides to rump and tail. Female has sharp, dark streaks on ginger-brown background, male less streaked, more chestnut on back, with grey head (brightest in summer) and red on head and breast (brighter and more extensive in spring). Light, twittering, chattering calls in flight, *tet-et-et*; typical finch nasal, rising *hooeee*; musical song.

HABITAT All kinds of open places with plentiful seed-bearing plants, chiefly in lowlands; in autumn and winter around gravelly edges of flooded pits, edges of saltmarsh, tidelines, and waste ground.

BEHAVIOUR A social finch, forming close, organized flocks. Feeds on ground; groups perch in bushes, singing in chorus.

Male ►
Unmarked
chestnut back; black
outer wings and tail
streaked white

◄ Tail pattern
White on tail evident from
above and below

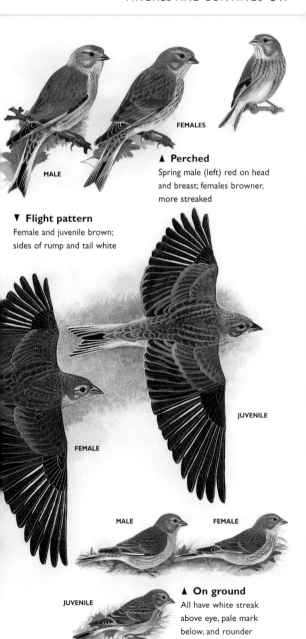

FEMALES

▲ Perched
Spring male (left) red on head
and breast; females browner,
more streaked

▼ Flight pattern
Female and juvenile brown;
sides of rump and tail white

MALE

JUVENILE

FEMALE

MALE   FEMALE

JUVENILE

▲ On ground
All have white streak
above eye, pale mark
below, and rounder
patch on cheek

Reed Bunting
Emberiza schoeniclus

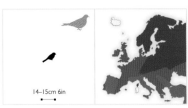

14–15cm 6in

DISTRIBUTION
Breeds near water
or on drier moors;
in winter in fields,
marshes, rough
ground near coasts,
rivers, and pools

Autumn male ▶
Fresh feathers have pale edges,
obscuring summer pattern beneath;
head pattern remains distinctive

Spring male ▶
Pale edges wear away,
gradually revealing richer
pattern, blacker
head and breast

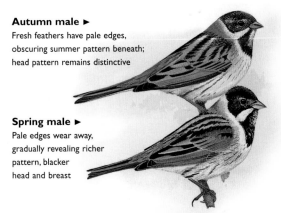

IDENTIFICATION A typical bunting, a little larger than most finches, with a sharp, triangular bill, a flatter head, and a longer, slimmer tail with broad white sides. Streaked black above, on various shades of red-brown and golden-brown; whiter below with short, sharp, dark streaks. Male easy to tell, with black on head and throat, extending to large bib in summer, and white moustache. Female more obscure, with dull head pattern, plain on crown and cheek, greyer on back of neck, a pale stripe over the eye, a broader creamy band beneath the cheek, and a thin, black moustachial streak widening out at the base of the neck. Calls include thin, sharp *see* and fuller, slurred *siu* or *syoo*.

HABITAT Mostly along waterside vegetation, also fields and marshy places in winter.

BEHAVIOUR Outside breeding season forms mixed flocks with other buntings, finches, and sparrows. Feeds on the ground, but often seen in low, waterside bushes, reeds, and sedges.

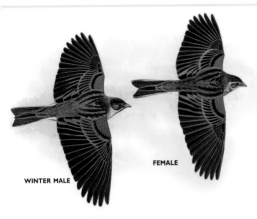

FEMALE

WINTER MALE

▲ Flight patterns
Looks quite broad-winged; longish tail often blackish; with clear white sides; flight low, flitting

Spring male ►
Pale edges wear off feathers to reveal clear black head and throat, white neck, blackish back, grey rump

Summer female ▼
Streaked black, cream, and rusty-brown; plain crown, dark cheek with slightly rufous centre, pale under cheek, dark moustache

Spring male ▲
Becomes much darker on back and tail than in winter

GREYER
FEMALE

WINTER
FEMALE

JUVENILE

Lapland Bunting
Calcarius lapponicus

15–16cm 6in

DISTRIBUTION
Scarce breeder on high ground and tundra in far north; migrants and scarce wintering birds on low-lying coasts

Spring male ▼
Eyecatching combination of red-brown-, black-and-white, with big rufous nape, black face, and pale, curved stripe around cheek

Winter female ▲
Broad rufous midwing panel; blackish edges to pale cheek; grey marbling on throat and breast

First winter female ▲
Heavily marked above; pale lines along back; orange-buff on nape; black cheek corners; rufous band on wing, edged white

First winter male ▲
Laplands all have short, dark legs (pale on reed bunting)

JUVENILE

▼ **Flight patterns**
Compact; shortish, dark tail;
upperwing has two white wingbars

FIRST WINTER

WINTER MALE

IDENTIFICATION   Easy in summer, both by plumage of male and location, but more of a challenge in winter. Looks somewhat like reed bunting, but its shape, short, black legs, and behaviour more like snow bunting. Look for pale centre to crown (dark on reed); bright rufous nape (duller on female, greyer on reed); pale stripes along back; blackish corners to cheek patch; broad central band of rufous on wing, edged by two thin white wingbars (plainer on reed). Calls include distinctive fast, low, hard rattle or trill (less musical than snow bunting), and short, sweet note, combined as *tr-r-r-r-r-r-t teu* or *ticky-ticky-tik tew*.

HABITAT   Breeds on tundra-like areas at high altitude, or lower down in the far north. In autumn and winter typically in rough, short grass near coasts, inner edges of saltmarsh. Migrants also on golf courses and similar open places close to the coast.

BEHAVIOUR   A ground-loving bird, rarely perching very high. Walks and shuffles on ground, looking low and hunched, not perching much in tall vegetation as does reed bunting.

SUMMER FEMALE

▲ **Tail patterns**
Adult (left half) has whiter sides than juvenile (right half), less clear than on reed bunting

Snow Bunting
Plectrophenax nivalis

Autumn juvenile female ▶
Dullest, least amount of white, but note white wingbar patch on inner wing; rufous cheek and crown

Summer male and female ▼
Male black and white; female (right) more streaked, greyer above and on head

16–18cm 7in

DISTRIBUTION Rare breeder in Scotland, more common Iceland, Norway; winters on hills, moors, coasts around North Sea

IDENTIFICATION A long, low, short-legged bunting, variable in detail. In summer extensive black-and-white obvious, even on female. Autumn and winter coastal migrants may be bewildering, but essentially show black legs, yellow bill, round head with rusty-orange crown and cheek, white chin and throat, rufous breastband, white or buffish underside. In flight reveals dark wingtips and greater or lesser amount of white on inner wing. Calls include liquid, stuttering, or rippling trill *p-rr-rr-r-r-it* and loud, musical *tyoo*.

HABITAT Breeds on high rocky mountains, screes, northern moors, and tundra. Migrants and winter birds on edge of saltmarsh, sandy or shingle shores, sometimes by reservoirs inland.

BEHAVIOUR Sometimes solitary, but winter birds usually in lively flocks of about 10 to 100 or more, feeding on the ground.

▲ Flight from below
Male has sharp black wingtips; paler on female and juvenile

◄ Winter male
Most extensive white in winter on oldest males; whole inner wing white, sides of tail white; rufous head pattern, yellow bill

◄ Winter
Juveniles and females vary, but show white wingbar or broad panel, black wingtips

▼ Winter adults
Adult female (upper) and male (lower) a rich combination of white, black, buff, and tawny-rufous in winter

▼ Winter females
Juvenile (upper) and adult variant (lower) buff-brown-, white-and-black; yellow bill; short, black legs

Index